Wings … chi

Peter R. Myers

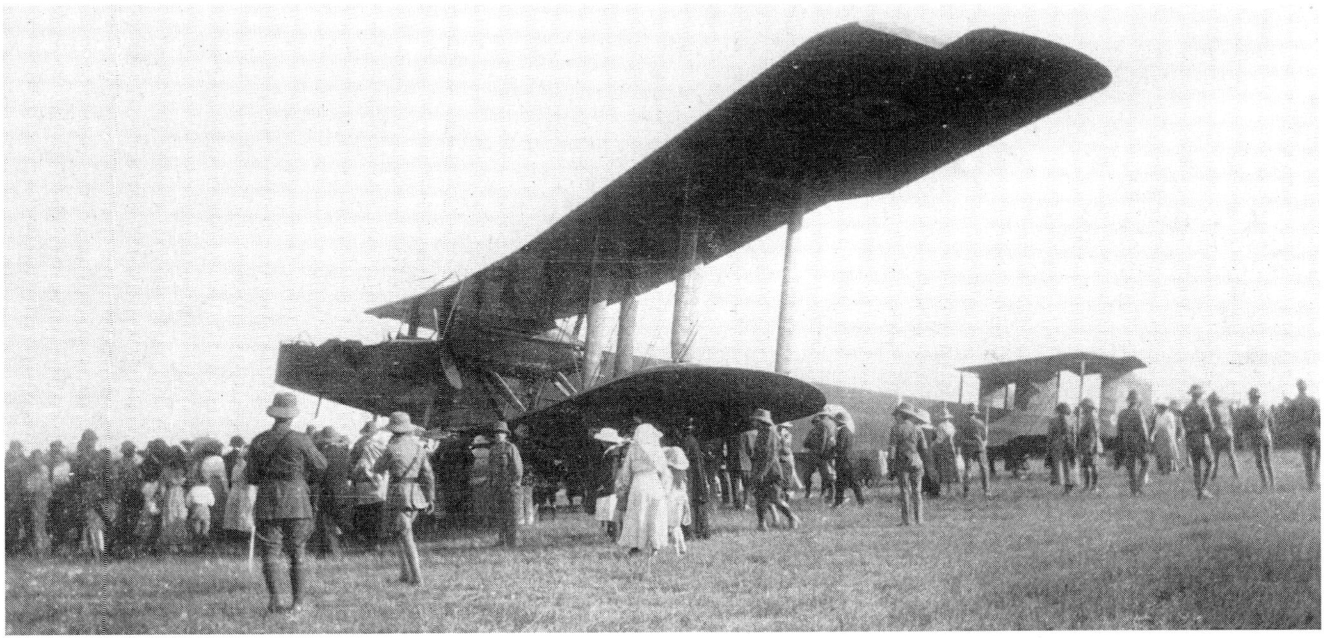

Handley Page O/400 C9681 is the focus of attention on 12th December 1918 after its arrival at Karachi following its flight from Egypt. The aircraft had left Heliopolis on 29th November and was flown by Captain Ross M. Smith of the Australian Flying Corps. He was accompanied by Brigadier General A.E. (Biffy) Borton, Major General W.G.H. Salmond, General Officer Commanding, RAF Middle East, and two other crew members. The Handley Page had routed via Damascus, Baghdad, Bushire, Bandar Abbas and Chahbar, and the total time spent in the air was 36 hours for the 2,548-mile journey. Salmond was to discuss with members of the government of India the organisation and establishment of the aerial route and service to India. C9681 had been the only aeroplane of its type in the Middle East and had been flown out from Cranwell, Lincolnshire, to Cairo at the end of July 1918 by Brigadier General Borton and Major A.S.C. MacLaren. On August 29th, Borton arrived at Ramleh with the Handley Page and it was put on the strength of No. 1 Squadron, Australian Flying Corps, which had distinguished itself in the war against the Turks in Palestine.

First published in the United Kingdom, 2020,
by Stenlake Publishing Ltd.,
54-58 Mill Square,
Catrine, Ayrshire,
KA5 6RD

Telephone: 01290 551122
www.stenlake.co.uk

Printed by
Blissetts, Roslin Road, Acton, W3 8DH

ISBN 9781840338775

Picture Acknowledgements

Chris Knott Collection: pages 15, 48, 49, 50, 51
Lawrence E. Massey via his son, Alistair Massey: pages 52, 53
The remaining photos are from the author's own collection.

Further Reading

R.E.G. Davies, *A History of the World's Airlines*, 1964
Paul Ellis, *British Commercial Aircraft, sixty years in pictures*, 1980
Sqn Ldr Tony Fairbairn, *Action Stations Overseas*, 1991
Selected Letters of T.E. Lawrence, edited by David Garnett, 1941
The Indian Air Force and its aircraft, edited by William Green, Gordon Swanborough and Pushpinder Singh Chopra, 1982
A.S. Jackson, *Imperial Airways and the first British airlines 1919-40*, 1995
K.A. Merrick, *Halifax, An Illustrated History of a Classic World War II Bomber*, 1980
Keith McCloskey, *Airwork, a history*, 2012
Fred Roberts, *Duxford to Karachi, An RAF Armourer's War*, 2006
Mansoor Shah, *The Gold Bird, Pakistan and its Air Force – Observations of a Pilot*, 2002

Periodicals

The Aeroplane
Aeroplane Monthly
Air Pictorial
Airliner World
Flight
FlyPast

Introduction

Karachi has a long and fascinating aviation history. From the 1920s until the dawn of the jet airliner era at the start of the 1960s, the city's airport and its military airfields were important staging posts for flights from Europe to India, south Asia, the Far East and Australia. The Royal Air Force established an aircraft depot at Drigh Road in 1920 and it was kept busy with the assembling and overhauling of RAF aircraft in India until the end of colonial rule in 1947. KLM Royal Dutch Airlines was among the first operators to use Karachi as a staging post when it inaugurated its passenger service from Amsterdam to Batavia (now Jakarta) in June 1927. The long-distance fliers of the 1920s and 30s, including Jean Batten, Bert Hinkler and Amy Johnson, staged through Drigh Road on their solo flights to Australia.

A civil airport was opened near RAF Drigh Road and for many years it was dominated by the colossal airship hangar, which was never used for that purpose after the airship R101 was tragically destroyed by fire in which 48 people were killed after crashing near Beauvais, France, in October 1930 on its maiden flight to India. Plans for airship travel to the sub-continent were abandoned in favour of biplanes such as the de Havilland Hercules of Imperial Airways which brought the first air mail from Britain to Karachi in April 1929. Indian airline pioneer J.R.D. Tata began carrying the air mail from Karachi to other Indian destinations from 1932, and his Tata Air Lines was the forerunner of Air-India. Meanwhile, modern monoplane aircraft, such as KLM's Douglas-DC-2, began to make Imperial Airways' biplanes look quite antiquated, especially the Handley Page HP.42 although it was safe, comfortable and reliable.

Karachi assumed major strategic importance in the Second World War when many combat aircraft were assembled and air tested at Drigh Road before playing their part in the war against the Japanese. The RAF established a flying-boat base at Korangi Creek, which became the largest in south Asia, and in the postwar period was used by the British Overseas Airways Corporation for its flying-boat route to India. A new airfield was opened in 1942 at Mauripur, north-west of Karachi, to take the pressure off Drigh Road; its extensive dispersal space was used by both the RAF and the United States Army Air Force, particularly for transport aircraft. The RAF continued to use Mauripur as a staging post for aircraft flying to the Far East and Australia until the end of 1956 after which the Pakistan Air Force had full use of the base which was renamed PAF Masroor.

After partition, Orient Airways opened domestic routes from Karachi, Pakistan's capital, to the new state's other cities and also linked West Pakistan with Dacca in its east wing, which is now Bangladesh. Pan American World Airways' elegant Lockheed Constellations first flew from Karachi to New York in 1947 and later staged through the airport on the airline's round-the-world service. It was with the Super Constellation that the state-owned Pakistan International Airlines (PIA) flew its first international flight from Karachi to London in February 1955.

The de Havilland Comet jet airliner dazzled the aviation world with its speed, comfort and economy of operation, but a series of tragic accidents cast a dark shadow over the pioneering airliner's future. One of those fatal accidents befell a Canadian Pacific Comet at Karachi in March 1953 while on a delivery flight. It was concluded that, in the darkness and limited visibility, the captain had allowed the aircraft's nose to rise prematurely during the take-off run. He later realised and corrected this mistake and the Comet became airborne, but too late to avoid striking an obstruction on the airport boundary.

A more successful British-built airliner was the Vickers Viscount with which PIA launched its first turboprop service between Karachi and Delhi in January 1959. That year, the Pakistan Government appointed Air Commodore Malik Nur Khan as PIA's managing director and under his leadership the airline became the first in Asia to operate jetliners when a leased Boeing 707 inaugurated its maiden jet service from London to Karachi in March 1960.

The only occasion the author has landed at Karachi Airport was in January 1987 while en route to Manila. Security was extremely tight following the hijacking of a Pan American Boeing 747 by Abu Nidal terrorists four months earlier when 20 passengers were killed after the airliner was stormed by Pakistani commandos. An armed policeman stood guard at the foot of the air stairs while myself and a few Italian tourists inhaled the cool night air as we watched a Romanian-registered Boeing 707 and an Iraqi Airways' Ilyushin Il-76 taxying past.

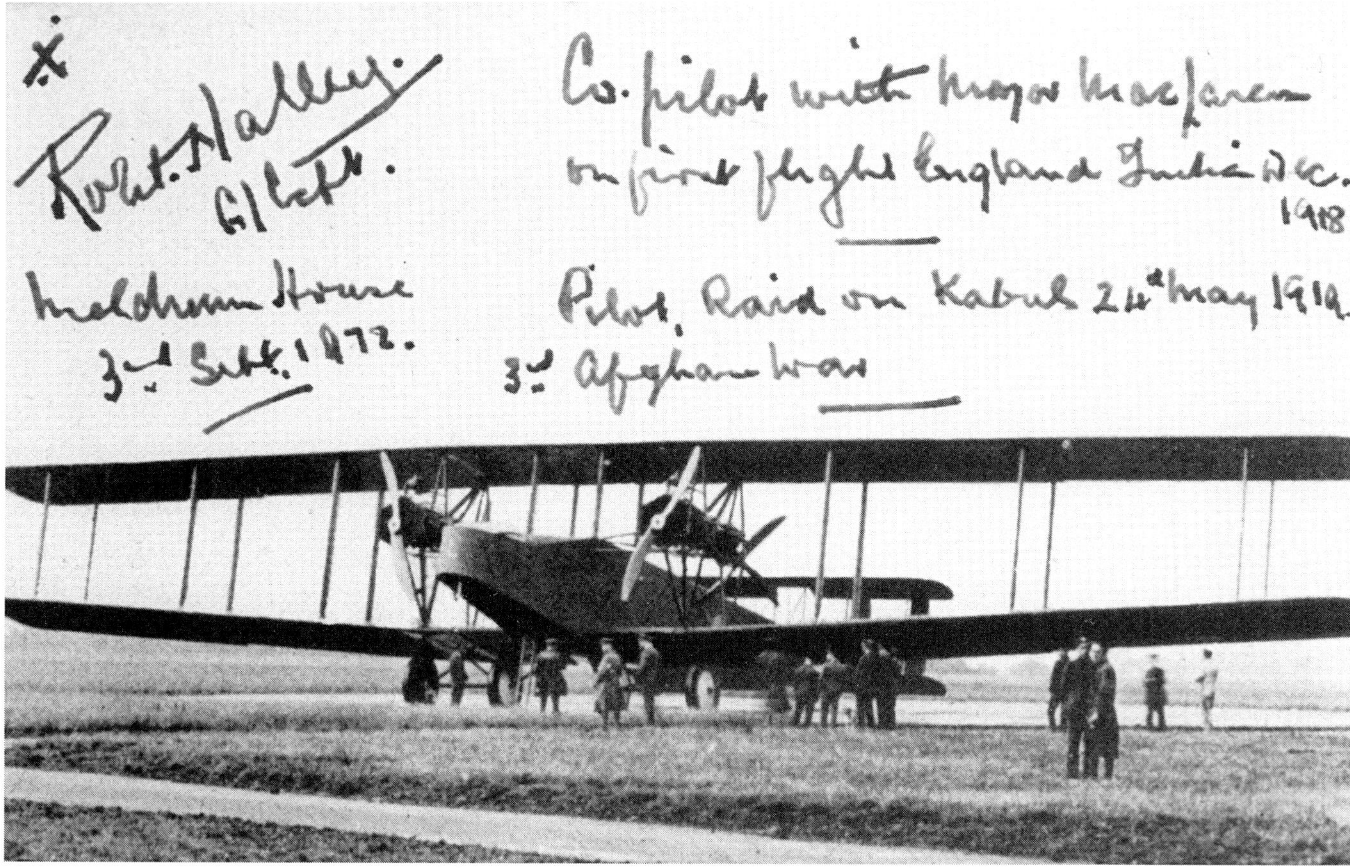

A photo of a Handley Page V/1500 signed for the author by Group Captain Robert (Jock) Halley, who was Major Archibald S.C. MacLaren's co-pilot during the first through flight from Britain to India in December 1918/January 1919. Flying such a big, unwieldy aeroplane as V/1500 J1936 was nothing short of epic and the journey was bedevilled by bad weather and mechanical failures. They left Martlesham Heath on 13th December 1918 and finally reached Karachi 34 days later on 15th January 1919. On the approach to Karachi, Halley related in an article in *Aeroplane Monthly* (December 1978) that they cleared a ridge with just a few feet to spare and made "a good landing with both engines full out". He recalled: "What a wonderful feeling of relief pervaded us when the aircraft came to rest intact. We quickly got out and danced with joy, hugging each other and going through antics which must have appeared to the crowd a very odd performance." Halley, a Scotsman, praised their three "stalwart" NCO mechanics – fitters Flight Sergeant Smith and Sergeant Crockett and rigger Sergeant Brown – for maintaining the huge aircraft as well as refuelling it at every stop with 1,000 gallons of petrol by means of four-gallon cans poured through a chamois leather funnel filter.

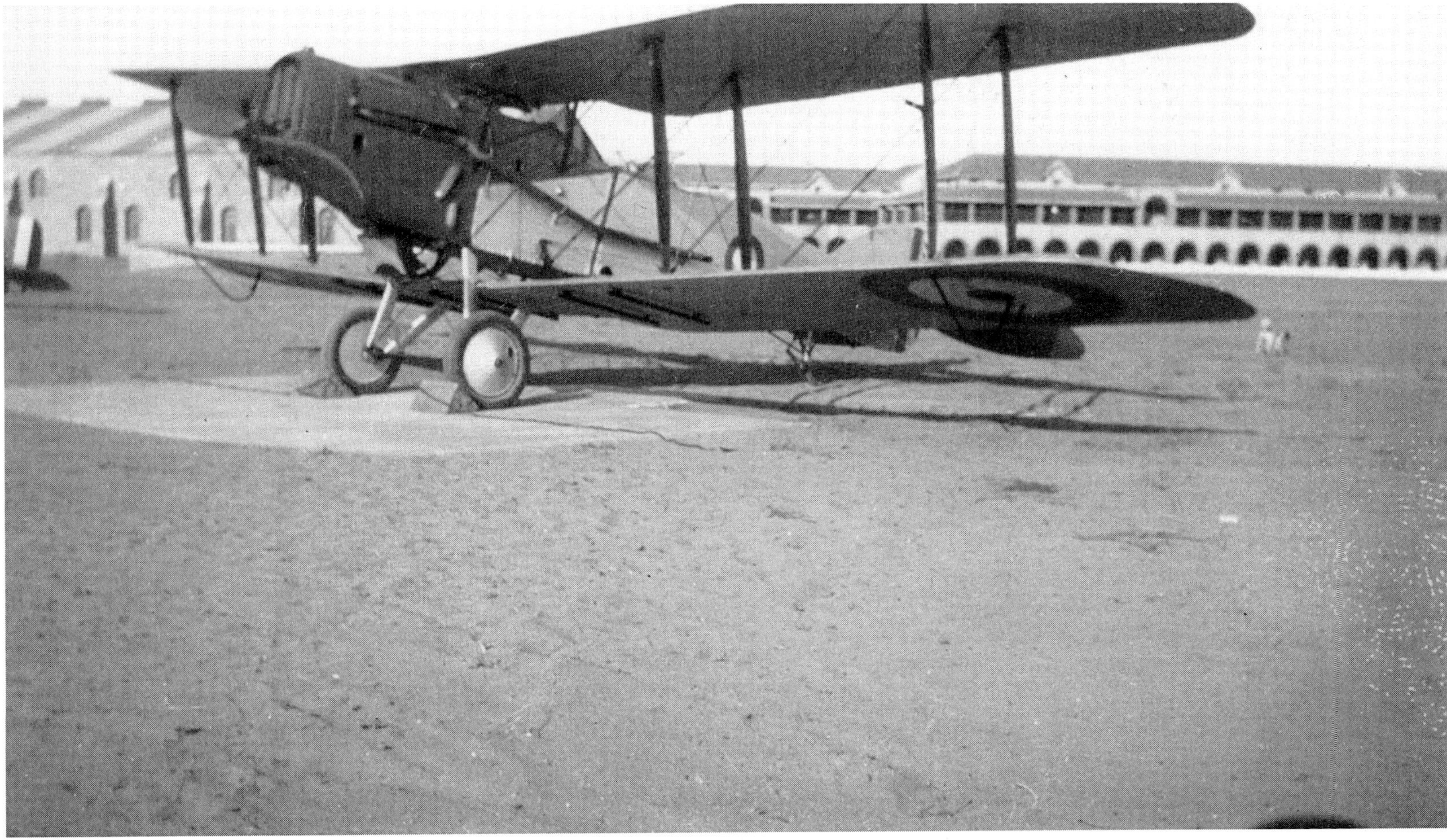

A Bristol F.2B Fighter at Drigh Road in the 1920s. T.E. Lawrence (Lawrence of Arabia) served in the engine repair shop at the Drigh Road Aircraft Depot, which had been established in 1920. In his collected correspondence it is only rarely that he mentions the nature of his work there. In April 1927, he tells a friend in a letter: "They have found me a job, in workshops. I follow the overhauling of each engine, as its particles float about the benches, and write a history of its new parts and processes. Tricky, and not either quick nor easy to do. Especially for a non-technical man, very vague as to the functions of a camshaft or inclined drive." He described Drigh Road as "a dry hole on the edge of the Sind desert … Over it blow hot and cold winds, very heavily laden with dust". Lawrence, who called himself T.E. Shaw during his second spell of service in the RAF, wrote to a friend: "Often in the evening I go out to the music of camel bells upon Drigh Road, and hang my topee on a cactus branch, and sit down under it, and weep, remembering Cranwell and the Great North Road."

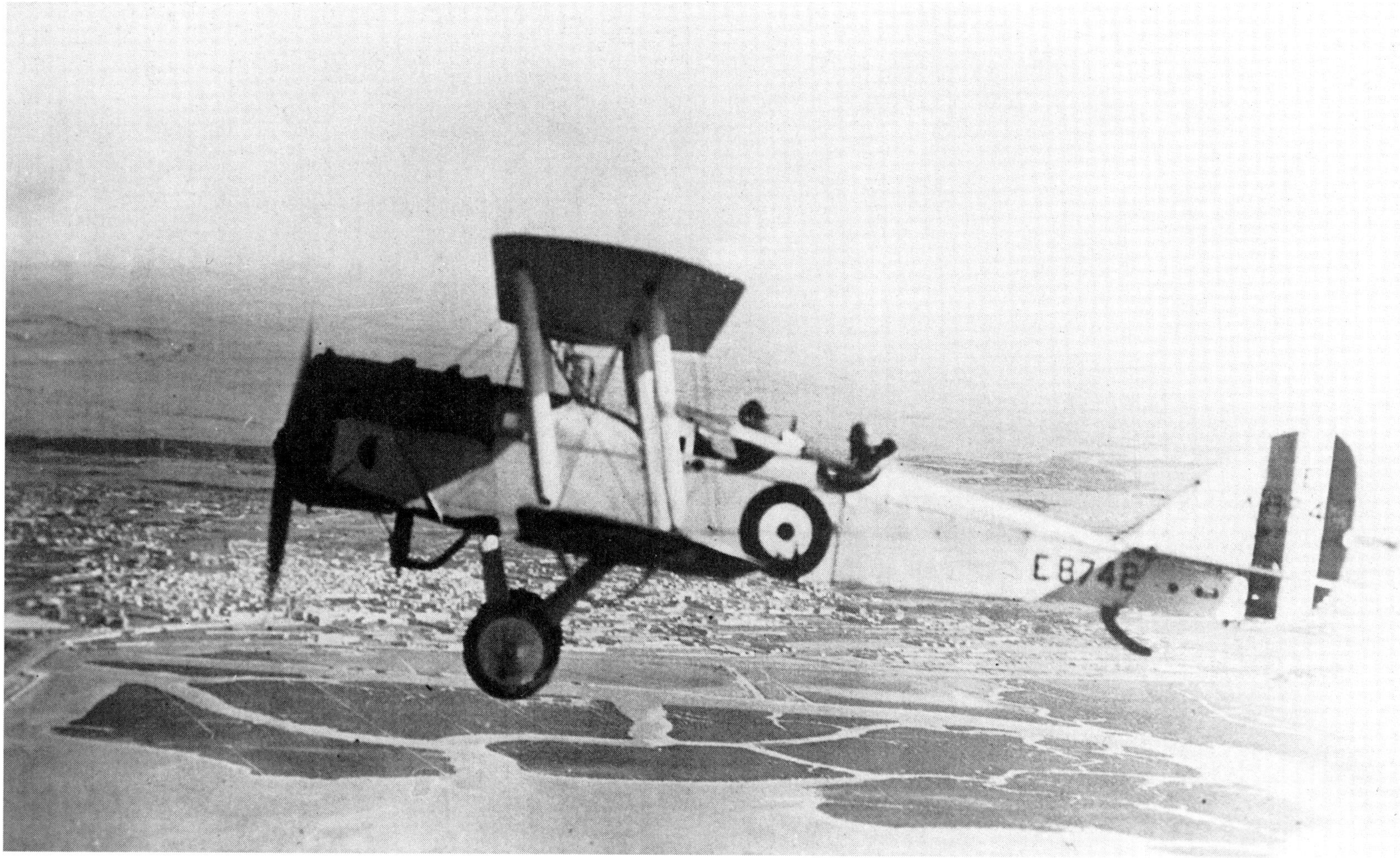

Airco DH.9A E8742 flying in the vicinity of Drigh Road in the early 1920s. The Aircraft Depot's location near the port of Karachi was a convenient one for the delivery of stores and crated aircraft for the RAF. The DH.9A, along with the Bristol F.2B and Westland Wapiti, were the stalwarts of operations over the North West Frontier and were a familiar sight at the air station. The versatile DH.9A, nicknamed the Ninak, first saw service during the First World War, and proved such a good aircraft that it continued in service with the RAF for 12 years after the war had ended. Its replacement was the Westland Wapiti which used many DH.9A parts.

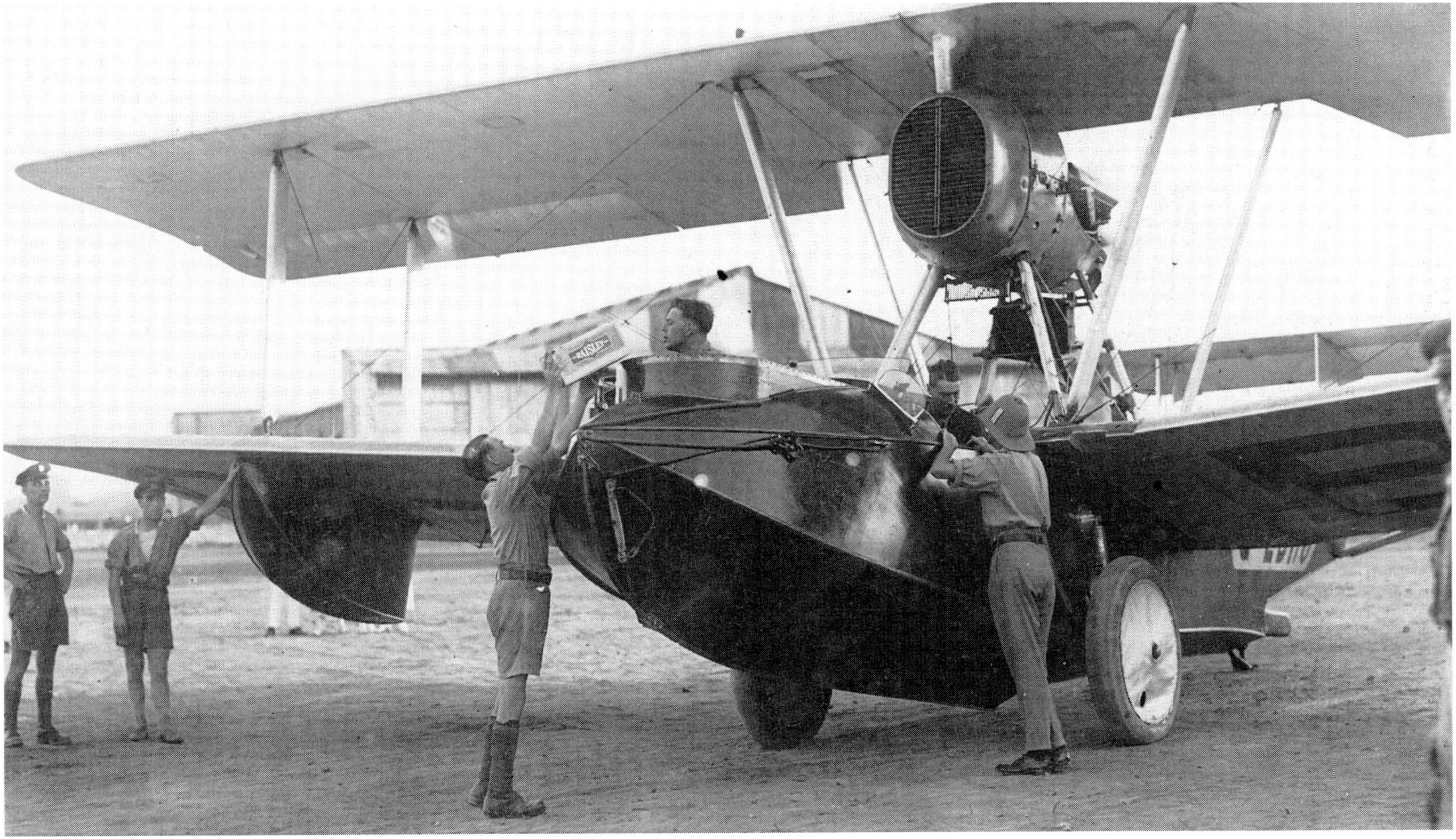

Squadron Leader Archibald MacLaren, the captain of the Handley Page V/1500 which made the first through flight from Britain to India in December 1918/January 1919, returned to Karachi five years later as navigator of Vickers Vulture I amphibian G-EBHO seen here at Drigh Road. He was the organiser of an attempted round-the-world flight with Flying Officer William N. Plenderleith as pilot and Sergeant R. Andrews as engineer. The Vulture was powered by a single Napier Lion engine and had left Calshot on 25th March 1924. The aircraft reached Akyab in Burma following two engine changes, but then crashed on take-off after being left uncovered in monsoon conditions for two days. The journey was then continued using the reserve Vulture I, G-EBGO, but unhappily this crashed in the Bering Sea near Nikolski off the coast of Siberia in thick fog on 2nd August, and the attempt was abandoned.

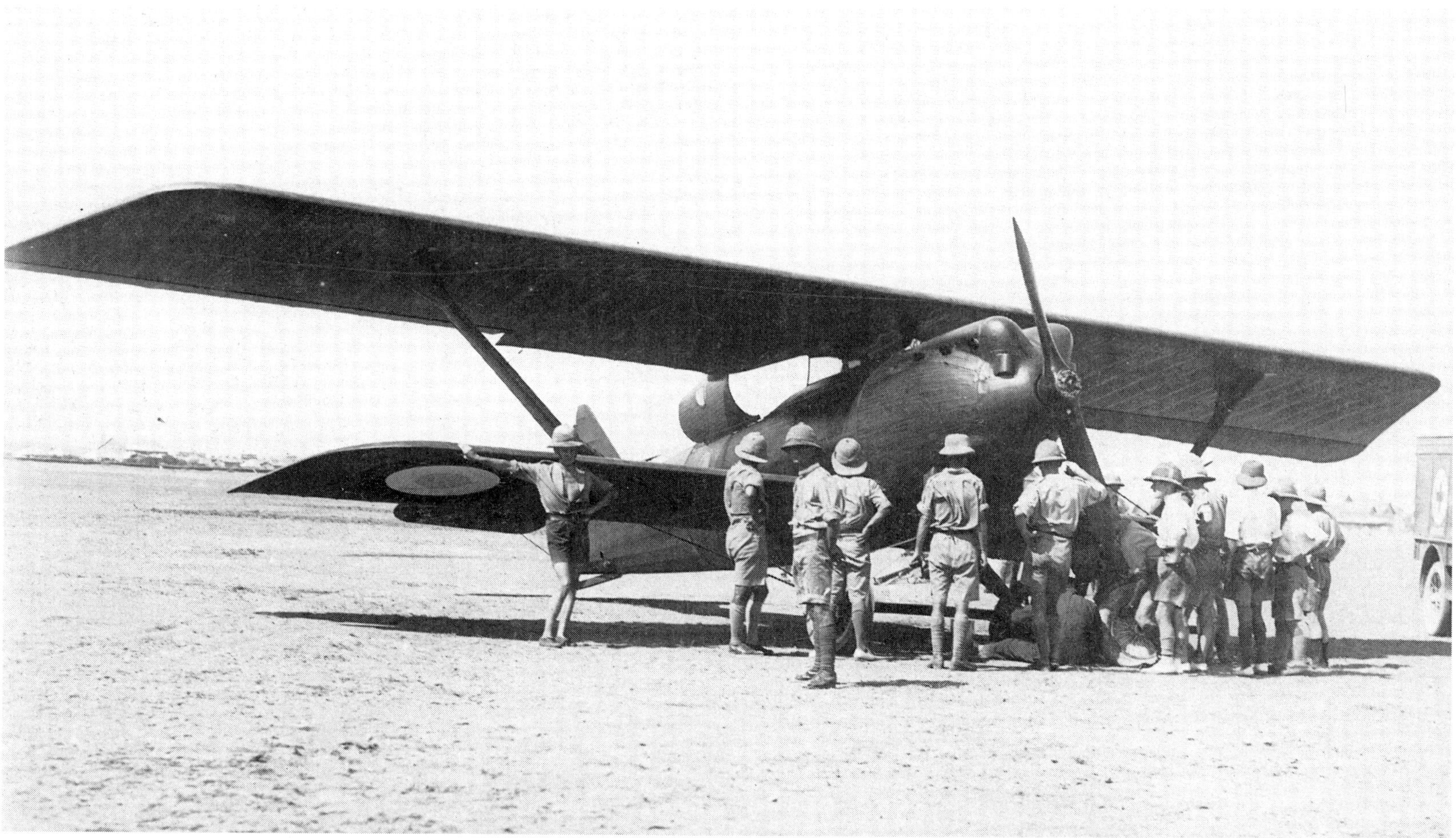

RAF airmen closely inspect a French Air Force Breguet 19.A.2, which had landed at Drigh Road on 29th April 1924. It was flown by Lieutenant Georges Pelletier d'Oisy and Adjutant Lucien Besin, who were attempting to fly around the world, having departed from Paris on 24th April. Their staging points on the flight to Karachi were Bucharest, Aleppo, Baghdad, Bushire and Bandar Abbas. They departed from Drigh Road on 3rd May and continued east to China via Agra, Calcutta, Rangoon, Bangkok and Saigon. Their attempt to circumnavigate the globe ended when they crashed their aircraft on a golf course in Shanghai after flying a distance of 10,580 miles in 26 days. While in Hong Kong, Pelletier d'Oisy met Squadron Leader MacLaren and Flying Officer Plenderleith who were attempting to fly around the world in a Vickers Vulture amphibian. Soon after that encounter Pelletier d'Oisy borrowed a Breguet 14 from the Chinese government and flew to Tokyo where he arrived on 17th July 1924. His total flying time from Paris to Tokyo was 120 hours spread over 84 days.

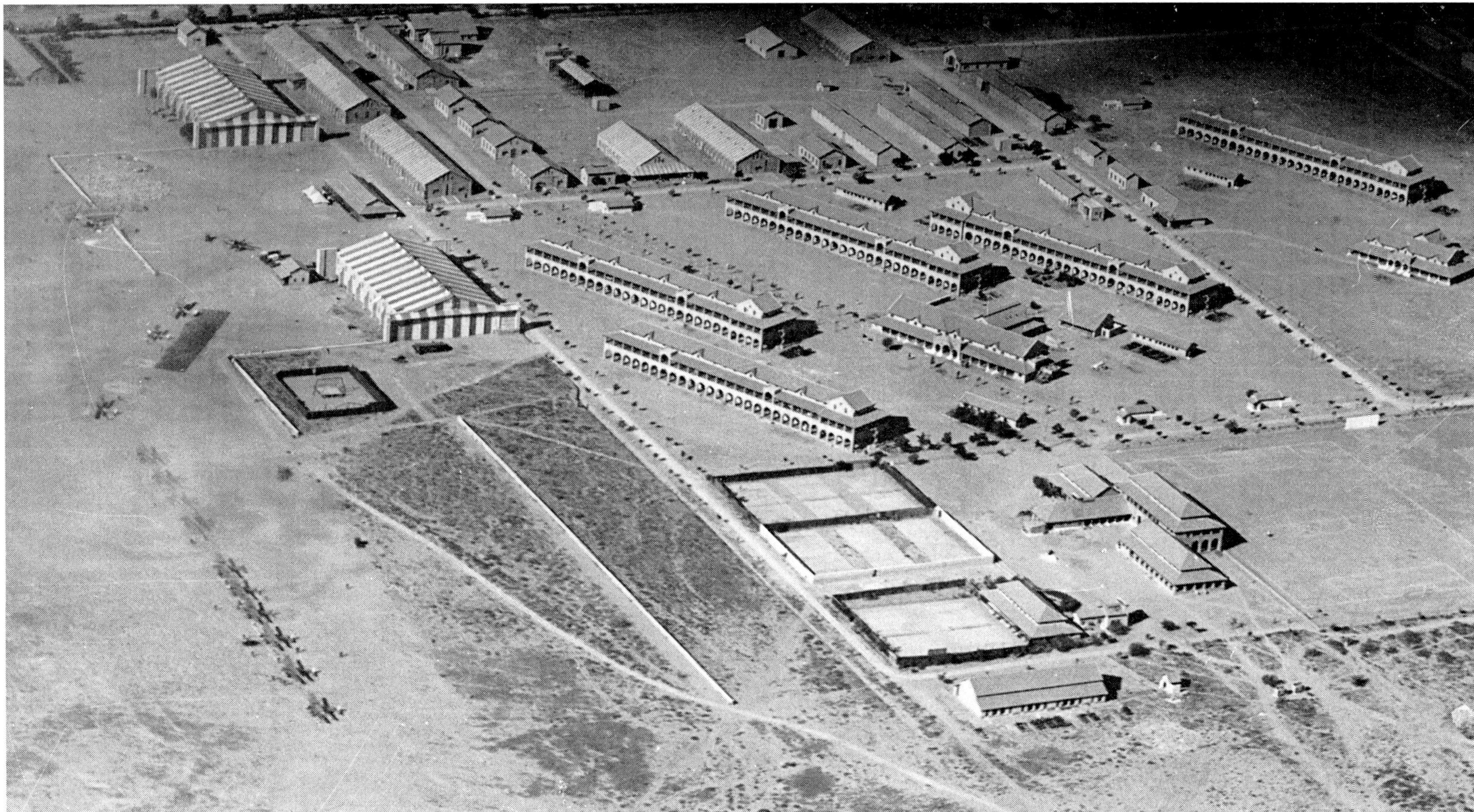

An aerial view of RAF Drigh Road in the 1920s. It was established as an aircraft depot in 1920 and its task was the assembly and overhaul of RAF aircraft in India, a role it performed during its entire existence. It was known initially as Karachi Depot but later became Drigh Road Depot, taking its title from Drigh Road Railway Station which was on the Karachi-Hyderabad line. The nearby port of Karachi was convenient for the import of stores and crated aircraft. Drigh Road may have had a dry and dusty appearance but was a welcome sight to aviators making long-distance flights to the Far East and Australia. Jean Batten, a New Zealander, staged through Drigh Road during her record-breaking solo flight from Britain to Australia in 1934. She had attempted the same journey the previous year in a de Havilland Moth but when she was approaching Drigh Road the engine blew itself apart suddenly and she glided down towards a long, straight main road. She was too late in spotting the white posts which bordered it and the Moth somersaulted high into the air, coming down on its back. Fortunately, she crawled unhurt from the plane's wreckage that marked the end of her first flight.

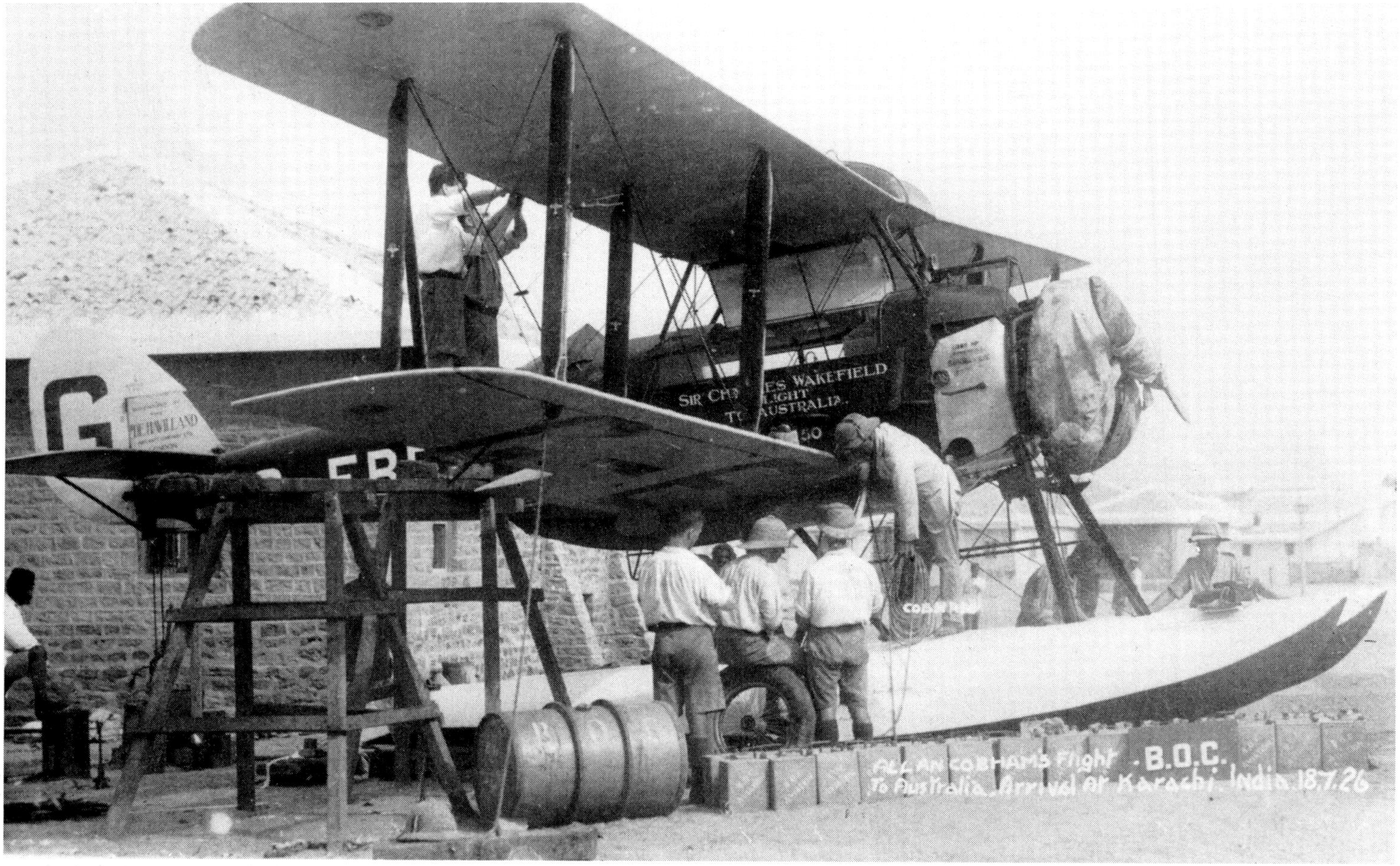

Pioneer long-distance aviator Alan Cobham made the first return flight between Britain and Australia in de Havilland DH.50 G-EBFO between 30th June and 1st October 1926. Cobham can be seen standing on a float while supervising RAF ground crew checking over the DH.50 at Karachi on 18th July during the outward journey. Cobham had taken off from the River Medway at the start of his epic flight but, tragically, engineer Arthur B. Elliott, who maintained the DH.50's Armstrong-Siddeley Jaguar engine, was shot and killed after they left Baghdad on 5th July. When they reached Australia, the DH.50's floats were removed at Darwin and replaced by a conventional undercarriage to allow Cobham to land at Essendon Aerodrome, Melbourne, where 60,000 people greeted his arrival. At the end of the return flight, Cobham landed on the Thames opposite the Houses of Parliament and was received on the Terrace by the Speaker of the Commons. Cobham was knighted soon afterwards.

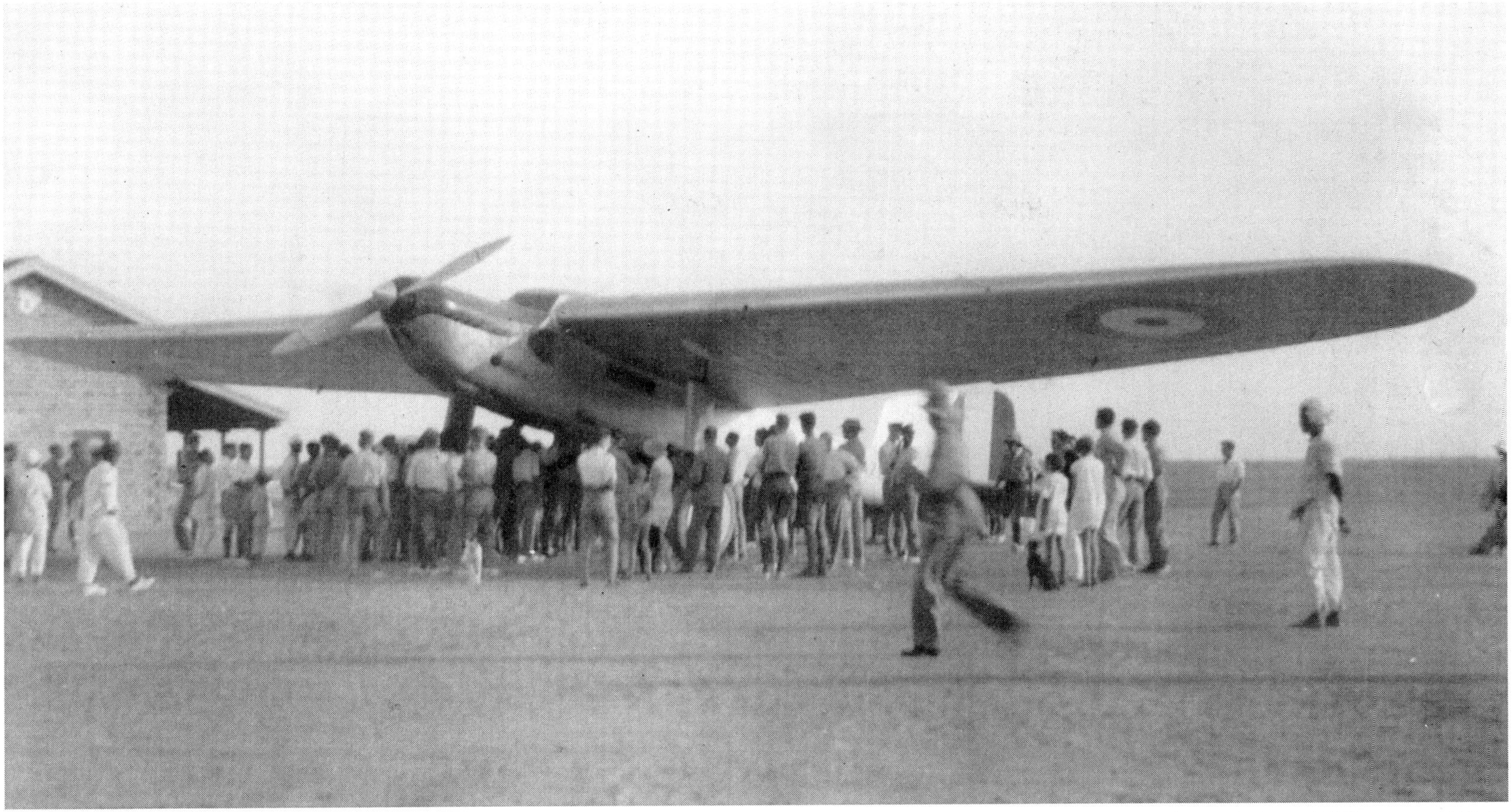

A crowd gathers round Fairey long-range Monoplane J9479 at Karachi on 25th April 1929 after its crew, Squadron Leader A.G. Jones-Williams and Flight Lieutenant N.H. Jenkins, had made the first non-stop flight between Britain and India. The aircraft was designed and built by Fairey at the invitation of the Air Ministry, which wanted to make an attempt on surpassing the distance record of 4,466 statute miles held by Italy. Jones-Williams and Jenkins took off from RAF Cranwell, Lincolnshire, on 24th April. They settled down to a routine of five hours on, five hours off, which they changed later to two and two. They encountered strong headwinds from Baghdad onwards which forced them to fly at lower altitudes. Karachi was reached just over 48 hours after leaving Cranwell. The crew set course for Bangalore but after an hour decided to turn back to Karachi because headwinds had taken their toll of the remaining fuel and they were afraid of having to make a night landing in the Western Ghats mountain range. They landed at Karachi after being airborne for 50hr 37min. Their Great Circle Distance was 4,130 miles, 336 miles short of the record, but they had achieved the first non-stop flight from Britain to India at a time when mail carried by Imperial Airways took six days.

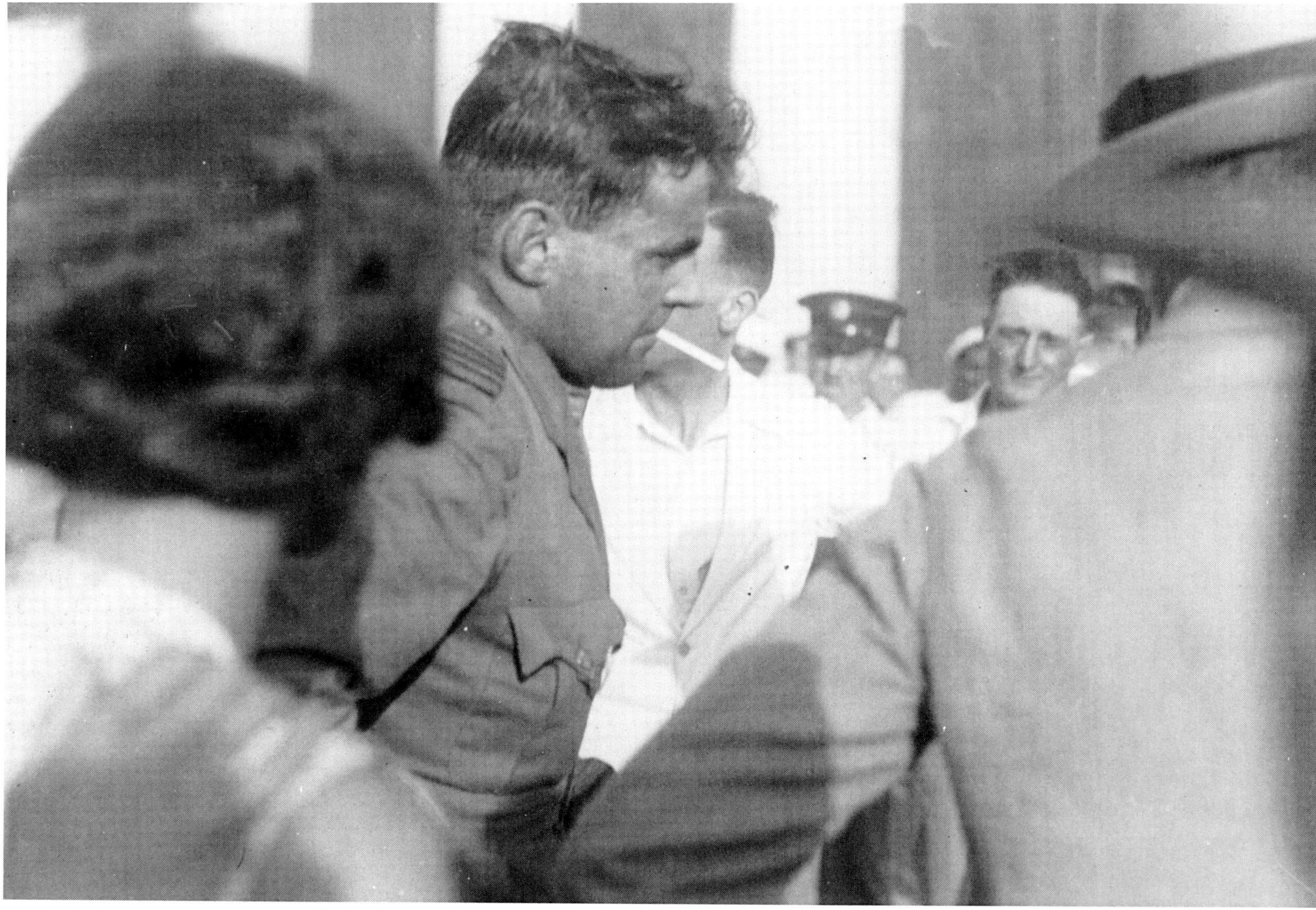

A rather dishevelled Squadron Leader Jones-Williams is interviewed after the epic flight.

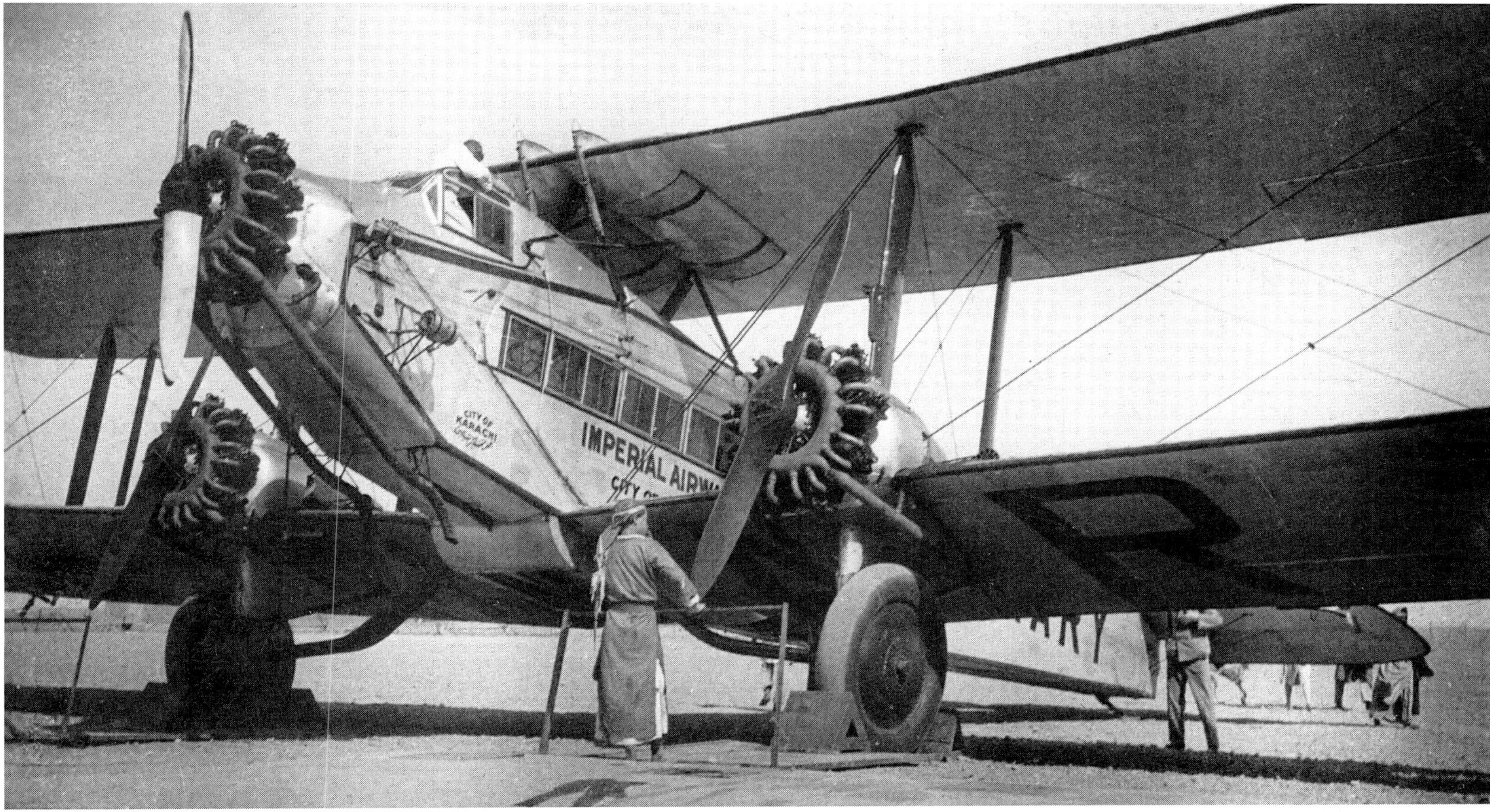

G-AARY, a de Havilland DH.66 Hercules of Imperial Airways and named *City of Karachi*, is seen at an airfield in the Middle East while operating the airline's Egypt-India service in the early 1930s. The Hercules was designed especially for the Alexandria-Karachi section of Imperial Airways' service, having ample power to cope with hot conditions and short airfields. The crew comprised of two pilots and a steward; seven passengers and nearly 500 cu ft of mail could be carried. Sister-aircraft G-EBMZ *City of Jerusalem* brought the first air mail from Britain to Karachi on 7th April 1929. In an article in *Flight* magazine (2nd April 1954), Maxwell Taylor recalled his air journey from London to India, being one of the route's first passengers in 1929. It was at Alexandria that he transferred to a Hercules "which had sliding windows and it was quite possible, at the expense of having one's eyes and ears filled with sand, to put one's head out of the window". The final hop was from Jask, Persia, to Gwadar, Baluchistan, and then on to Karachi, "where we arrived dirty, tired and almost deafened by the noise of the Hercules' three engines, heard only too clearly through the not-too-well fitting windows and the plywood-and-fabric fuselage walls".

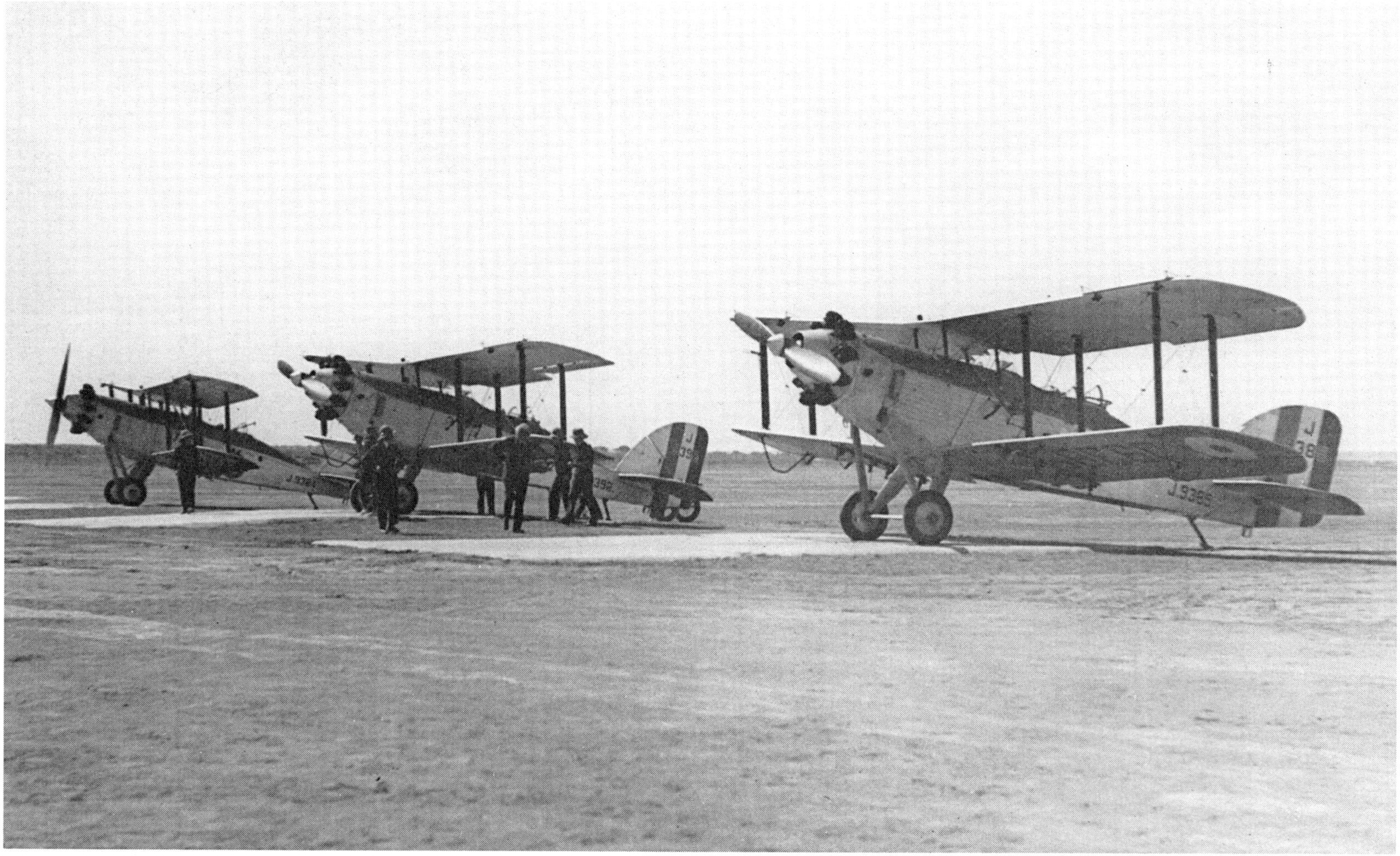

A trio of RAF Westland Wapiti IIAs lined up at Drigh Road. In November 1936, all squadrons based in the North West Frontier detached flights to Drigh Road for a three-week armament training camp where live bombing and air-firing practices were carried out against armoured target boats off Manora. The exercises proved timely because the Wapitis of Nos. 5, 27 and 60 Squadrons were soon in action against the tribal followers of Haji Mirza Ali Khan, the self-styled Fakir of Ipi, who had launched a jihad or holy war against the British in Waziristan.

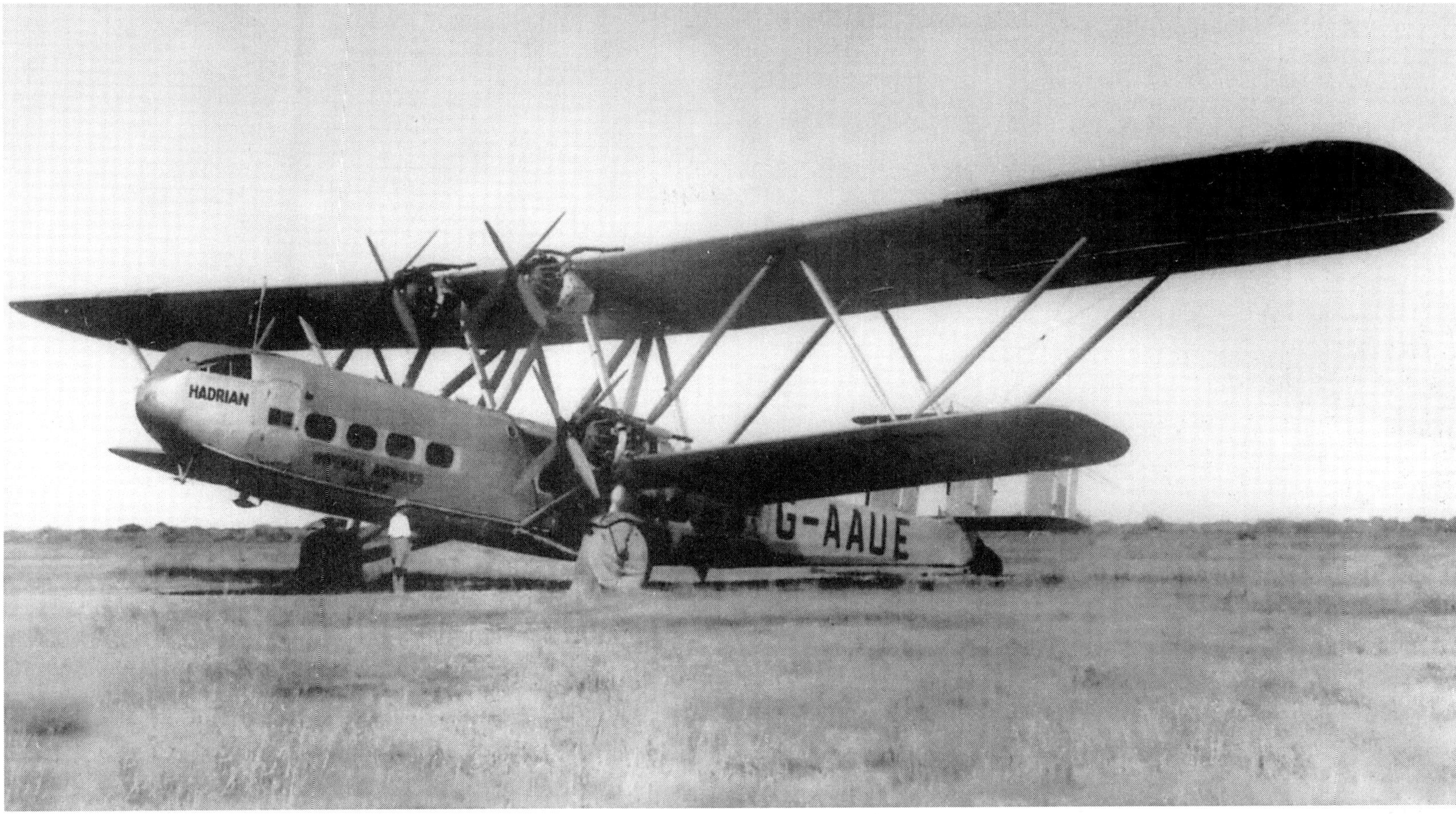

Handley Page HP.42E G-AAUE *Hadrian* of Imperial Airways at Karachi in 1935. The HP. 42 of 1931 was designed for Imperial Airways to succeed its Armstrong Whitworth Argosies and de Havilland Hercules, and offered superior Pullman-like comfort for the passengers. There were eight HP.42s of which *Hadrian* was one of the four Eastern type which accommodated 18-24 passengers and had twice the baggage space of the HP.42W (Western or European type). Passengers found they were quiet and comfortable, mainly because they sat well away from the noise of the four engines. However, they were handicapped by a slow cruising speed of 95mph which made them inferior to the fast monoplane airliners being developed in the US in the 1930s. The eight HP.42s operated largely without incident during most of that decade. The first to be lost was G-AAXE *Hengist*, converted to HP.42E standard in 1935 and destroyed in a hangar fire at Karachi in May 1937. During the Second World War, *Hadrian* was one of three posted to No. 271 Squadron RAF at Doncaster and bore the serial AS982 but was fated to be wrecked during a gale at Doncaster in 1940.

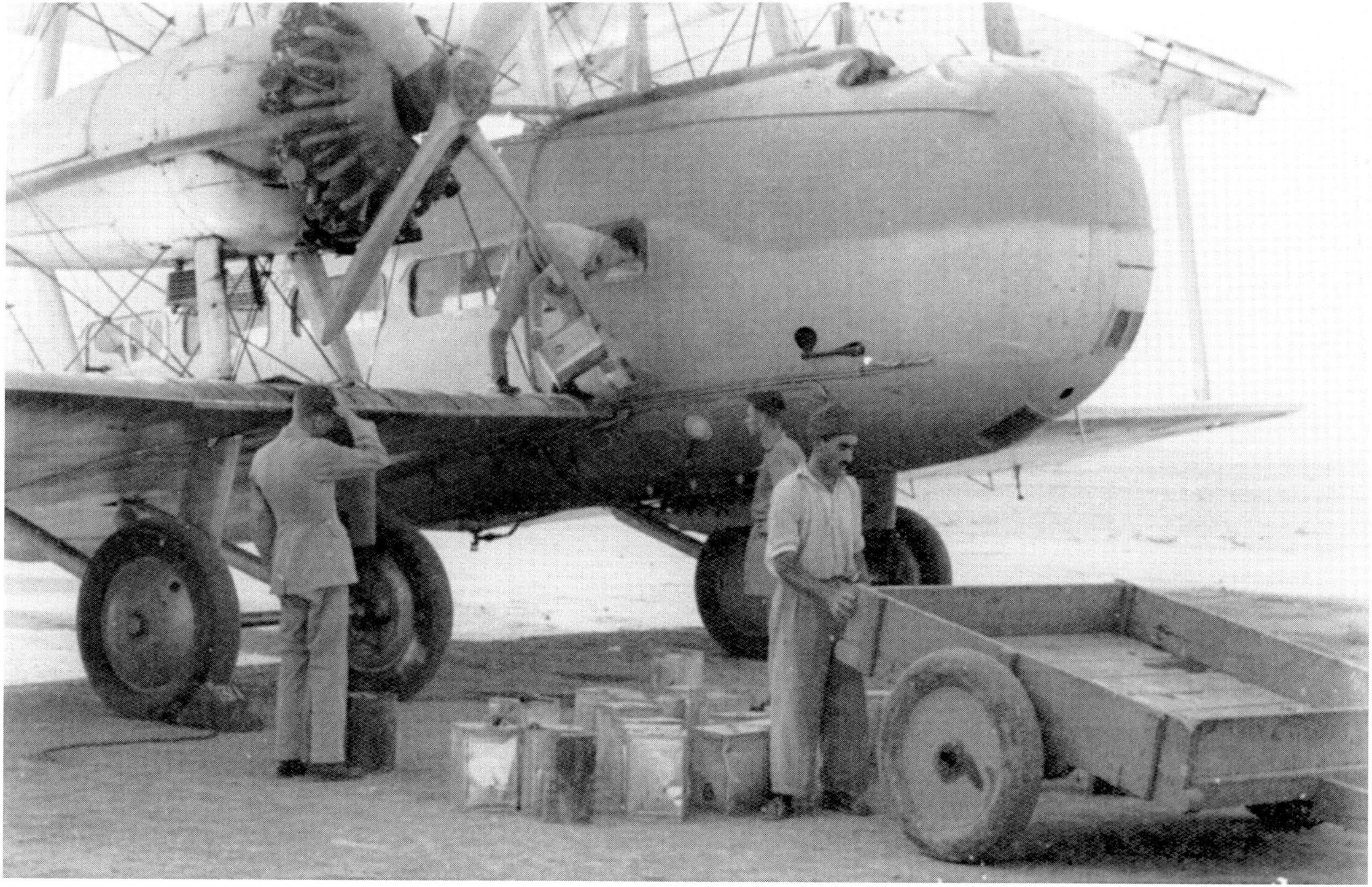

A Vickers Valentia is serviced at an airfield in India. These biplane troop transports/bombers of No. 31 Squadron were based at Drigh Road after moving from Quetta following the devastating earthquake there in May 1935. The squadron detached Flights to other places in India which included operations against dissident tribesmen. The squadron remained at Drigh Road until 1938 although it returned for a spell in 1941.

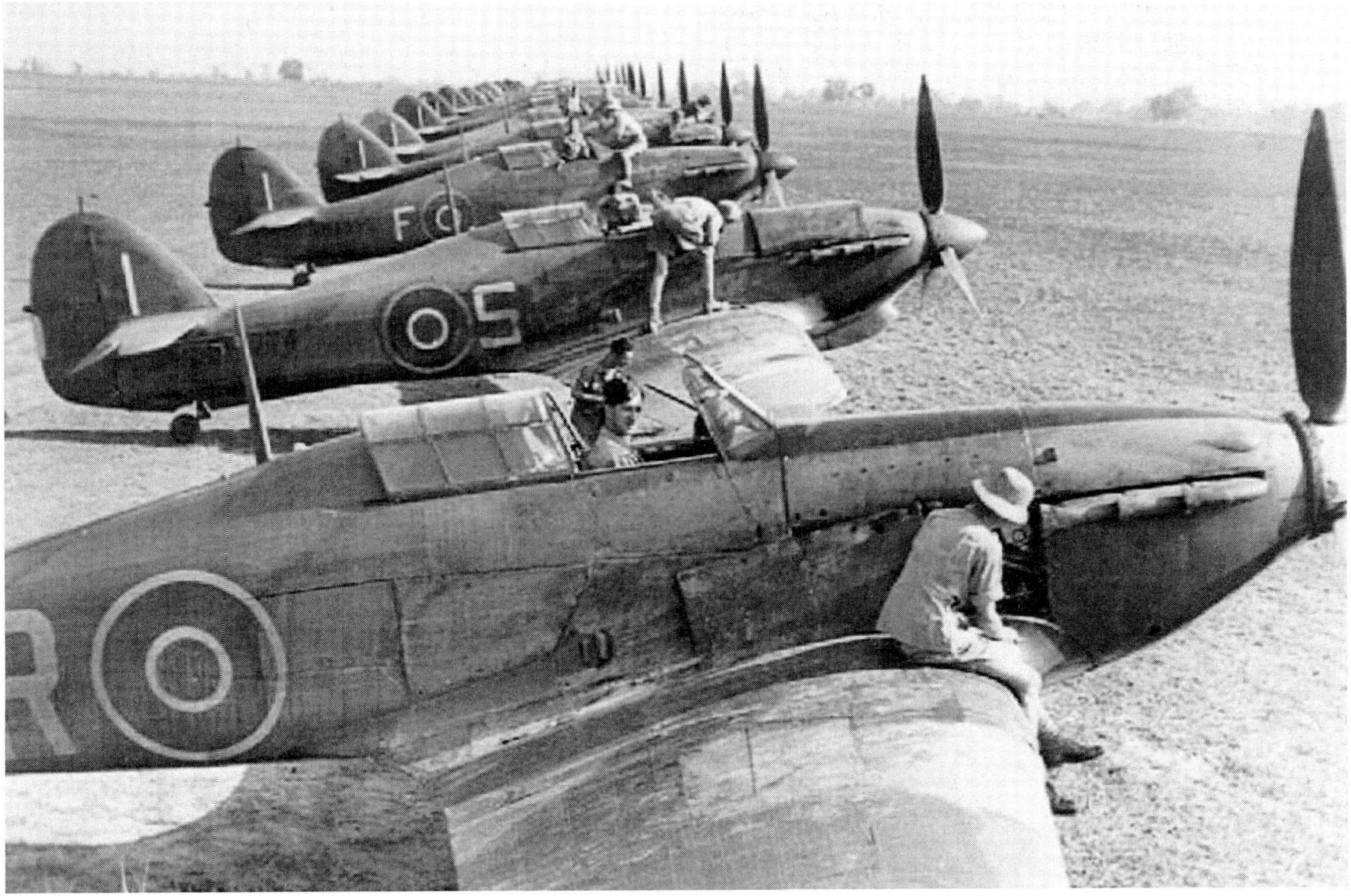

These Hawker Hurricane fighters of No. 67 Squadron, RAF, at Chittagong, East Bengal, c. 1943, had been shipped in wooden crates from Britain to Karachi, where they were assembled and prepared for operational service in south-east Asia at Drigh Road by No. 320 Maintenance Unit. Fred Roberts, who was an RAF armourer, served with this unit between December 1942 and February 1944, and in his book, *Duxford to Karachi*, he wrote: "The Hurricane guns and cannons were packed in separate wooden boxes inside the aircraft crates, four Browning guns or two Hispano cannons to a box. After removal of the guns or cannons, the boxes were broken up and burnt under a large steel vat of water. This was used to boil the cannons to remove the thick grease that covered them to protect them from corrosion. The Browning guns were washed in petrol to remove the grease. This work was carried out by the Gurkha labourers under the supervision of one of our LAC armourers. After de-greasing, the guns and cannons were stripped, examined and re-assembled by the armourers and then installed in the Hurricanes".

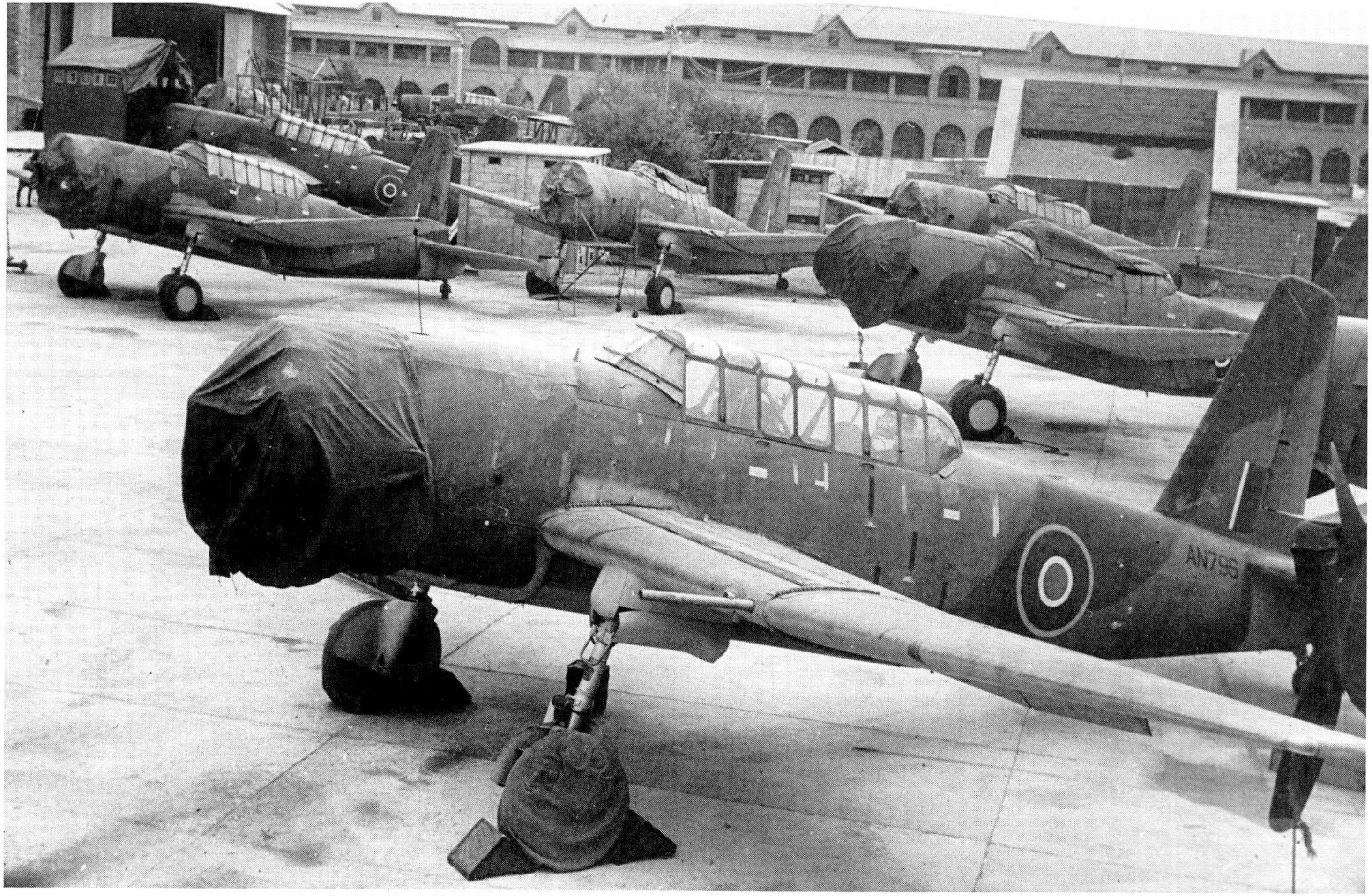

American-built Vultee V-72 Vengeance dive bombers await to be fitted with their propellers at Drigh Road, c. 1943. The aircraft had been shipped from the US to Karachi and then assembled at Drigh Road before being test flown. The Vengeance saw operational service in India and Burma with Nos. 45, 82, 84 and 110 Squadrons, RAF, as well as with Nos. 7 and 8 Squadrons, Indian Air Force. The type suffered numerous defects and teething troubles, requiring temporary withdrawal from the two IAF squadrons, but the snags were eventually mitigated if not eliminated. No. 8 Squadron flew its first operational Vengeance sorties against Japanese targets from Double Moorings, Chittagong, on 15th December 1943. No. 7 Squadron joined in sorties in the Arakan from an airstrip at Uderbund, near Kumbigram, where it arrived on 12th March 1944.

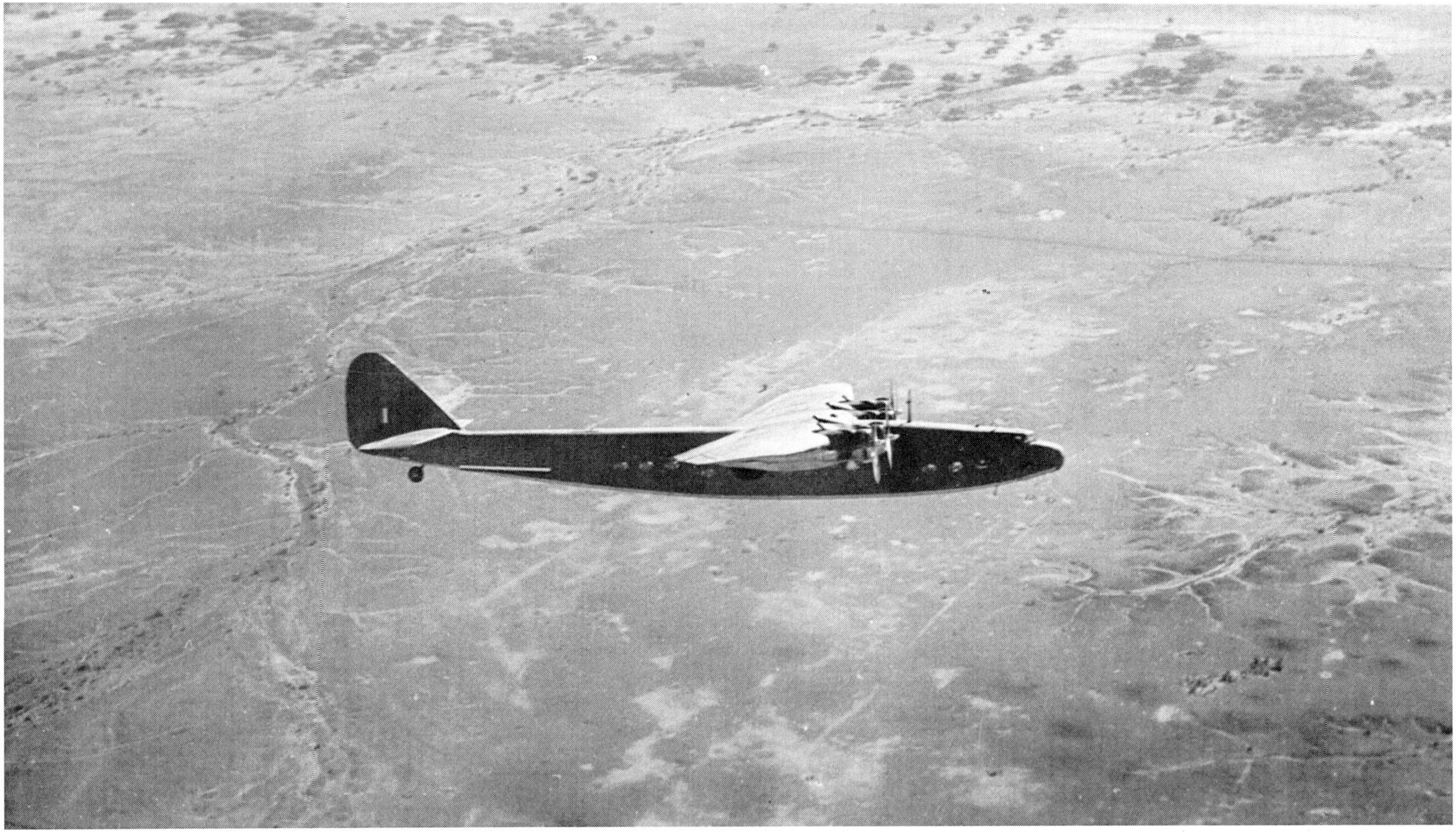

Armstrong Whitworth AW. 27 Ensign G-ADSV *Explorer* of the British Overseas Airways Corporation begins its descent before landing at Khartoum, Sudan, during the Second World War. Three of the first five Ensigns delivered to BOAC's predecessor, Imperial Airways, were used on a Christmas mail run to Australia in 1938 but they were bedevilled by problems with their underpowered Armstrong Siddeley Tiger radial engines, including G-ADST *Elsinore* which required an engine change at Karachi. Imperial Airways had intended that four of the Ensigns would operate from Calcutta with Indian Trans-Continental Airways but these plans were abandoned after the outbreak of war in September 1939. BOAC used its re-engined Ensigns on transport services in the Middle East and Africa, and in 1944 their services were extended to Karachi and Calcutta. After the war the Ensigns were flown back to the UK to be scrapped.

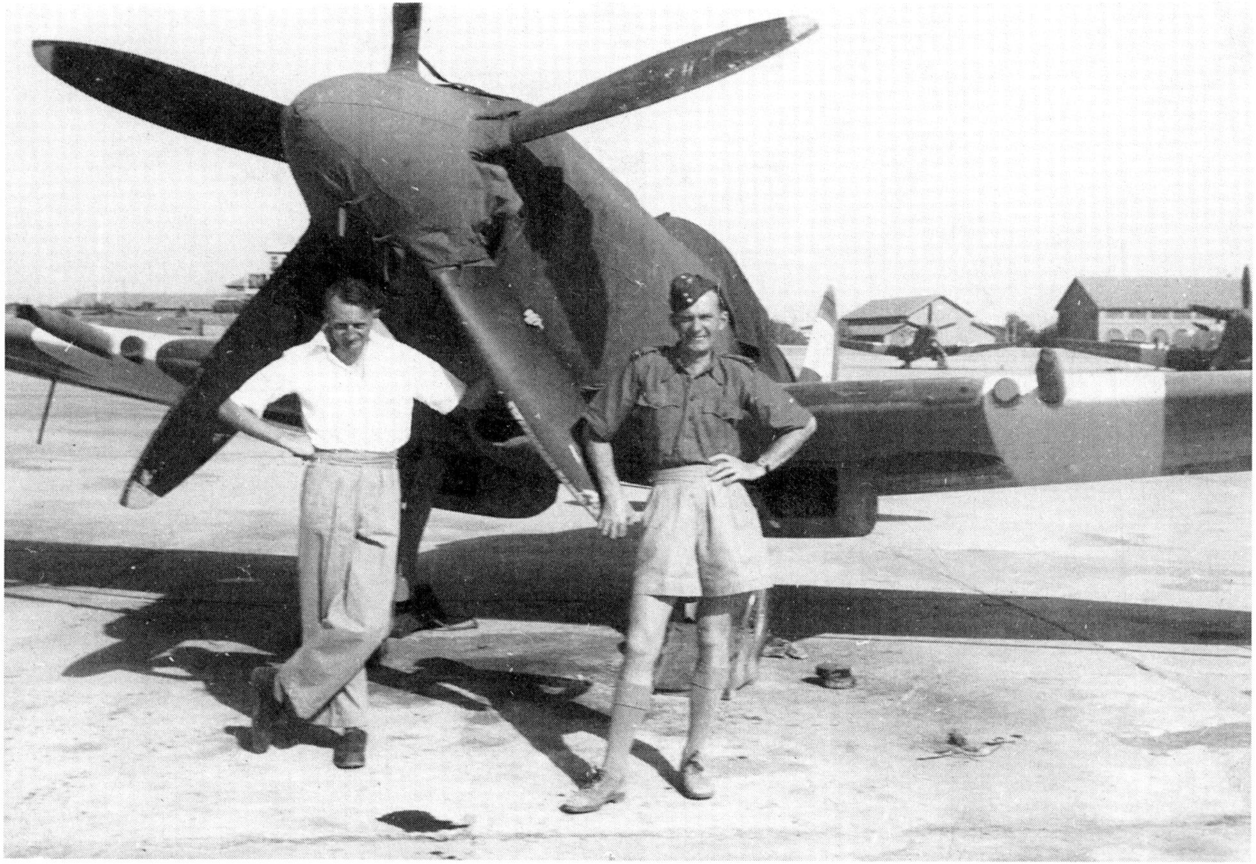

A Supermarine Spitfire, fitted with a five-bladed Rotol propeller, at Drigh Road in 1946. No. 320 Maintenance Unit continued to prepare Spitfires, particularly Mk XVIIIs, for service until 1947. C. Barrie Smith served as a flight test pilot at Drigh Road and recalled the work of No. 320 Maintenance Unit in an article in *FlyPast* magazine (November 1997). His logbook shows that he made a total of 223 test flights in Spitfire Marks Vc, VIII, IX and XI. He wrote: "At times there could be 60 to 80 aircraft there waiting to be serviced or being serviced. The ground crews worked under very hot conditions quite often and the aircraft became unbearable to handle. However, everything generally went very smoothly indeed." Test flying sometimes revealed unexpected faults which often resulted in an emergency landing. Smith recalls a particular incident when he was flying a Spitfire on an initial test. He smelt petrol and then the engine cowling burst open and flames came past the cockpit. Smith made a belly landing and "as soon as we came to a stop I was out and off. The fire petered out. On inspection it was found that a section of the carburettor had been improperly assembled by the manufacturers – a washer had been left out."

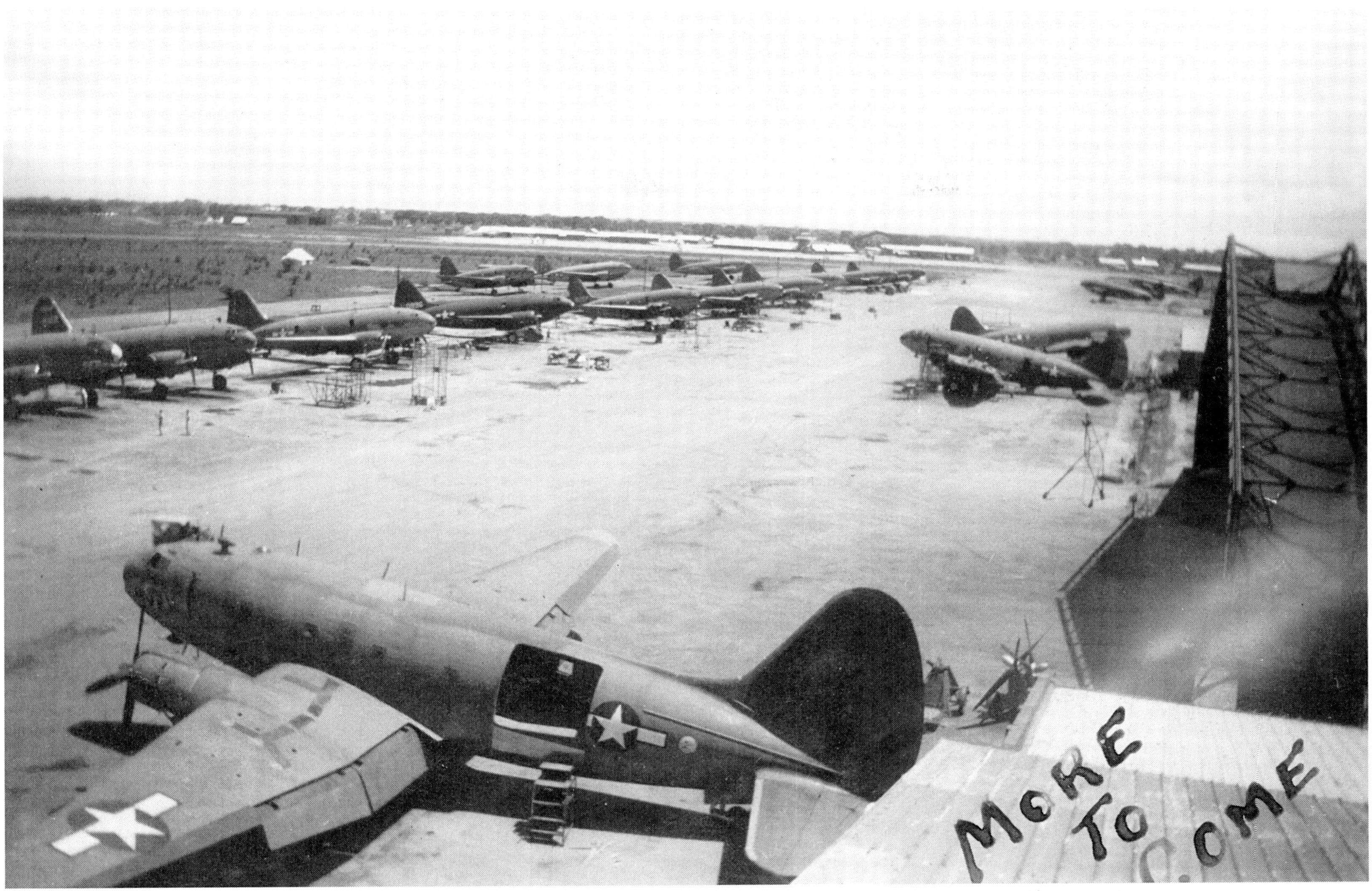

A wartime line-up of Curtiss C-46 Commandos of the Tenth Air Force of the United States Army Air Forces at RAF Mauripur, which was opened as a transit airfield in 1942 and had plenty of taxying and parking capacity. These C-46s would have flown supplies over the Hump from north-east India to Chungking, China, in support of US and Chinese forces fighting the Japanese.

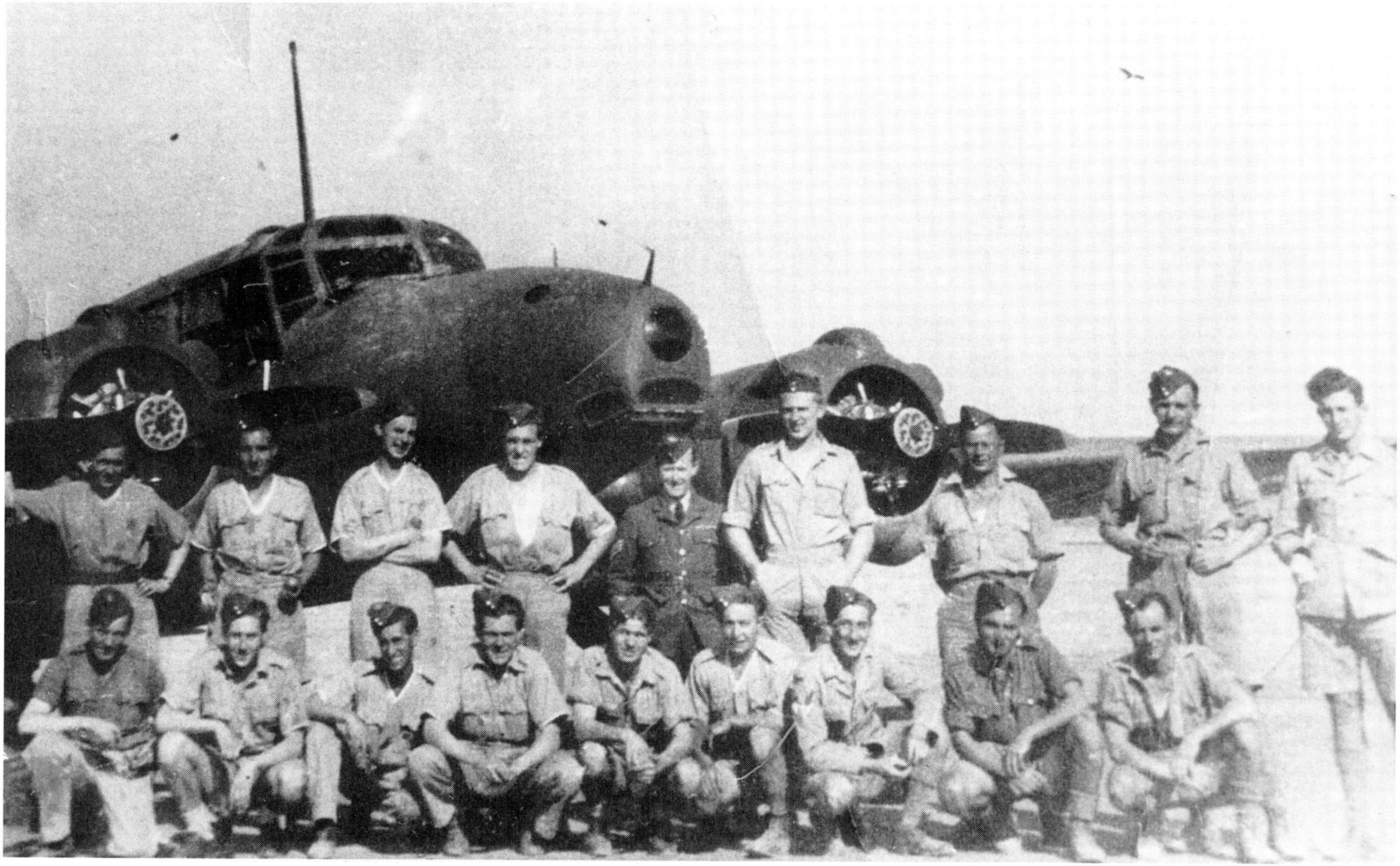

RAF airmen pose before Avro Anson Mk. I LT949 at Willingdon Airfield, New Delhi, in 1944. Ansons were assembled at Drigh Road before they were used in the training and transport roles throughout India in the Second World War.

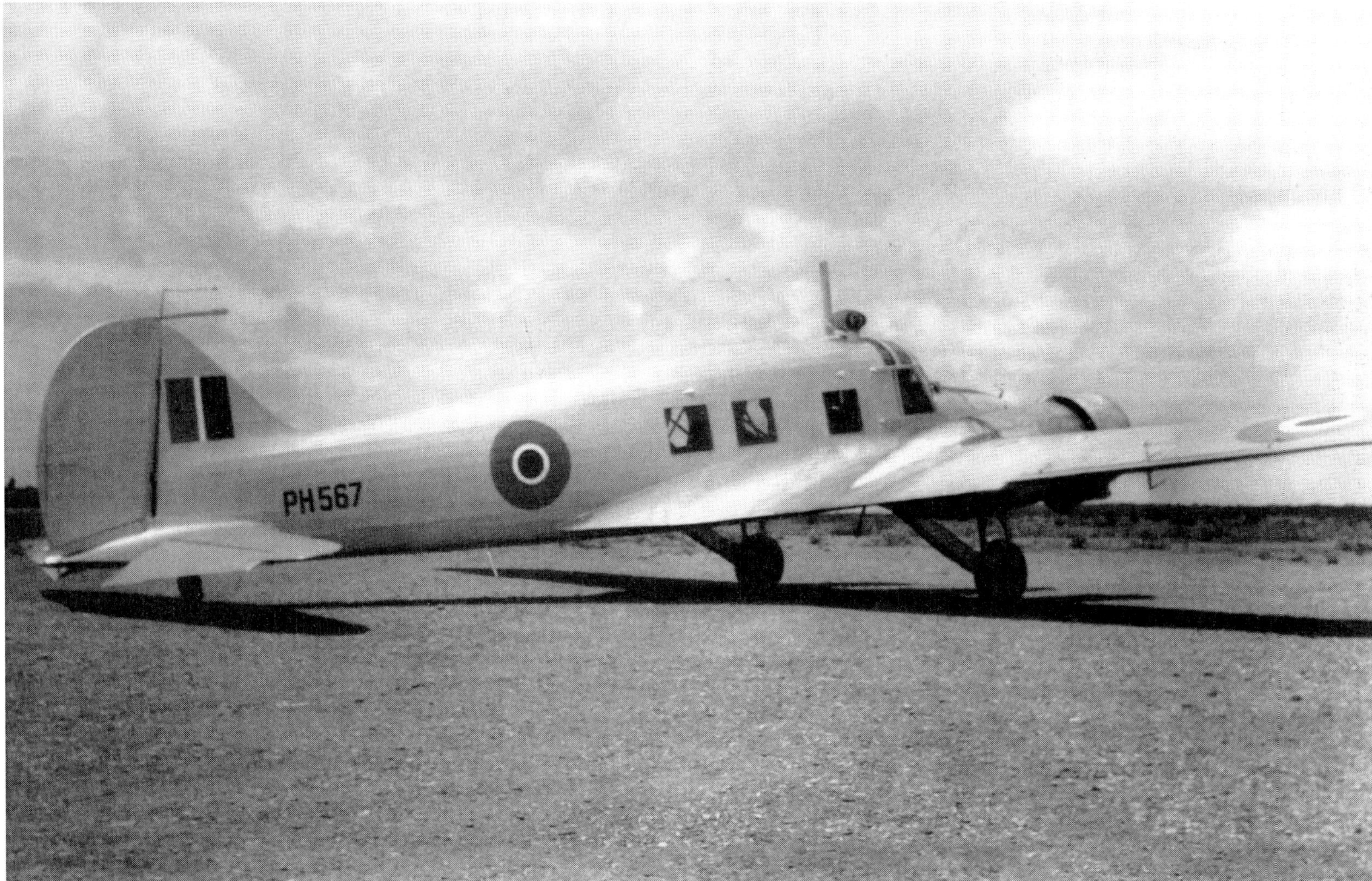

Avro Anson Mk. XII PH567 was flown from the Middle East to Karachi and Jodhpur in 1945 by the author's father, Ron Myers, while he was serving with the RAF's Middle East Communications Squadron, which was stationed at Heliopolis, Egypt. PH567, which was nicknamed Mighty Mouse, continued flying until struck off charge on 27th November 1947.

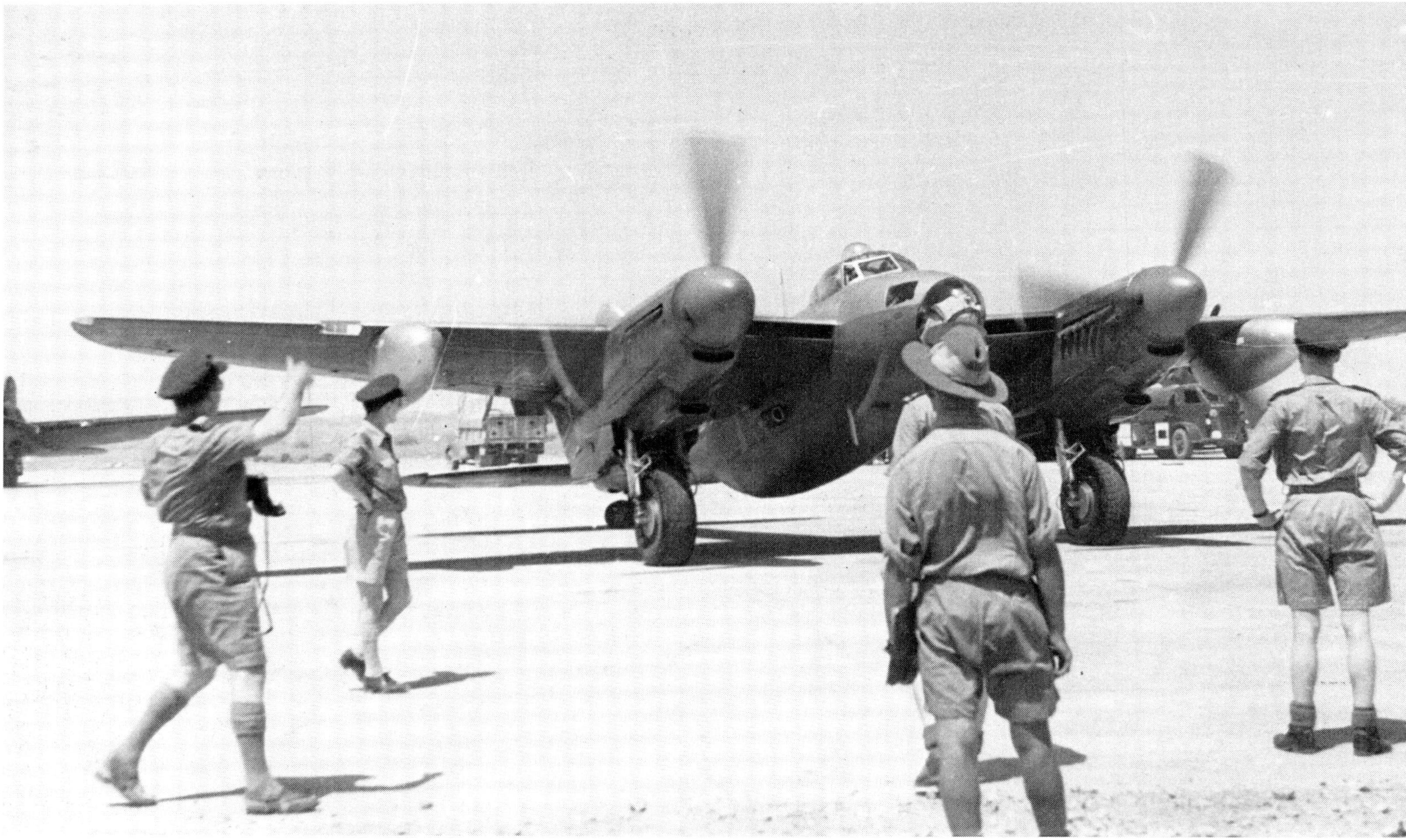

A de Havilland Mosquito PR.34 of No. 684 Squadron, RAF, arrives at Karachi after its record-breaking flight from RAF Benson, Oxfordshire, in June 1945. It had flown 4,700 miles, staging through Cairo, in the overall time of 12hr 25min at a mean average speed of 376mph. The pilot was Squadron Leader K.J. Newman, of Auckland, New Zealand, and his navigator was Warrant Officer R.E. Smith, of Chatham Green, Little Waltham, Essex. Three other photo-reconnaissance Mosquitos, which had left Britain a day earlier, also made the flight in less than 13 hours. No. 684 Squadron had been formed on 29th September 1943 at RAF Dum Dum, near Calcutta, and performed long-range photo-reconnaissance flights in support of the campaign in Burma. Near the end of the war the squadron also performed high-speed courier flights such as the one to Karachi.

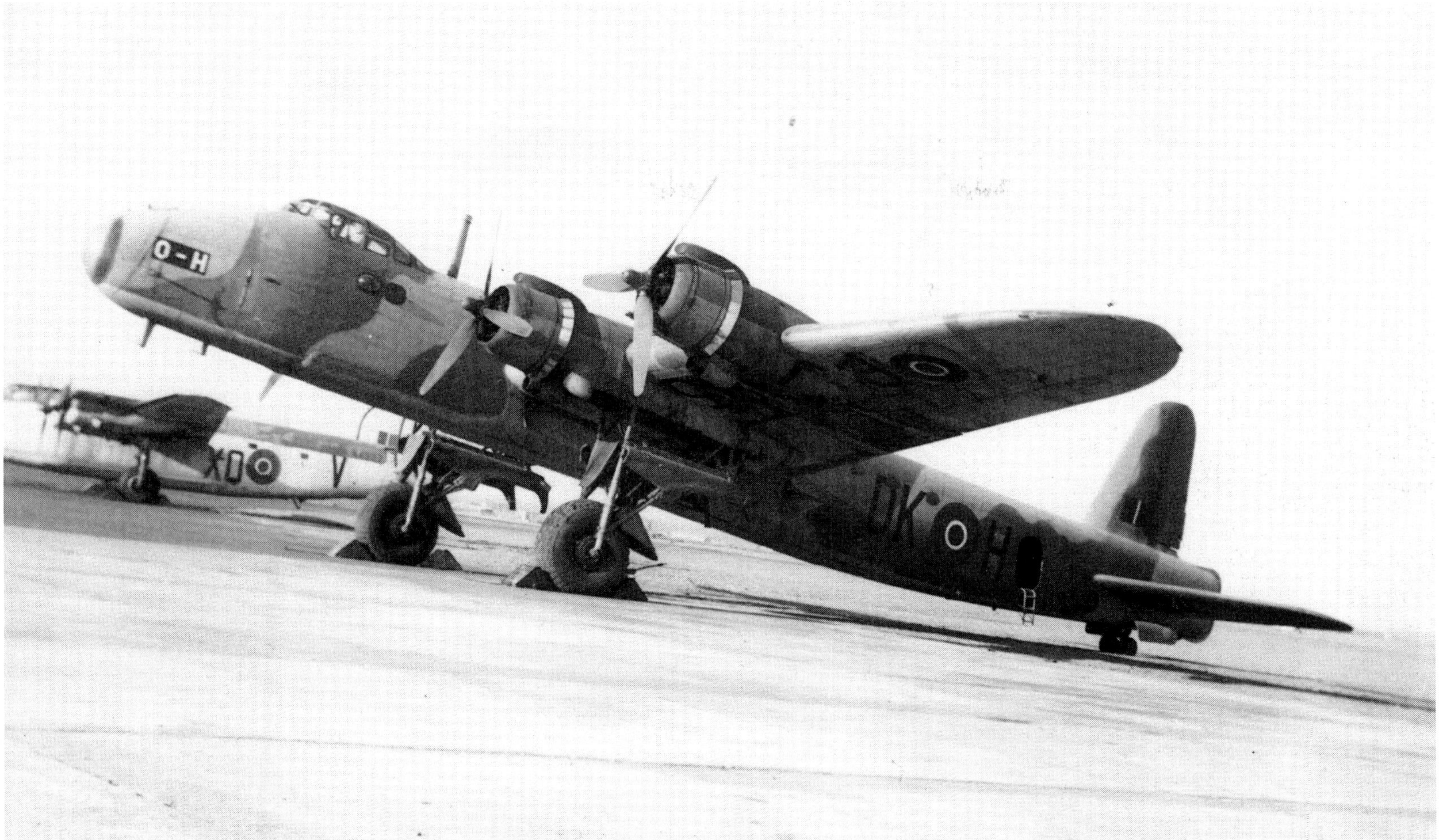

Short Stirling V PJ985 of No. 158 Squadron, RAF Lissett, Yorkshire, at Mauripur, in 1945. In *Short Stirling*, one of *Aeroplane Illustrated*'s 'Icons' (2015), Mike Pitchers recalls flying the Stirling V transport as a second pilot. He flew one on a return training flight from Lissett to Mauripur via Castel Benito, Lydda and Shaibah. The total flying time for the trip home was 28 hours, plus three overnight stops for rest and refuelling. On another flight to Mauripur their route was extended to Madras (Arkonam) which took more than six hours each way, "through the monsoon with rainwater dripping everywhere inside the aircraft". Their passengers for the return flight were all RAF personnel and all former prisoners-of-war, who "still looked very thin and ill, but they were glad that they were on their way home".

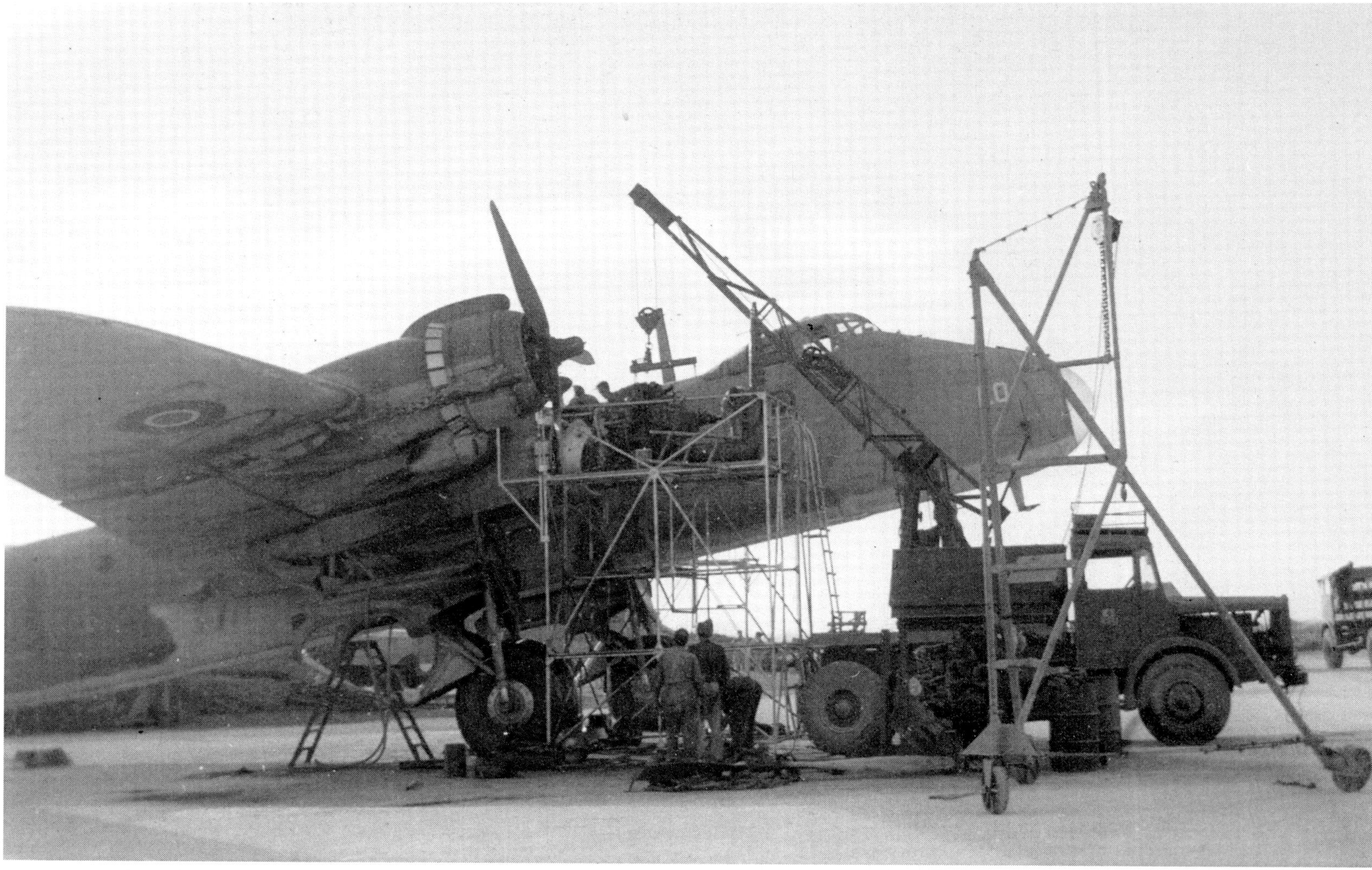

An RAF Stirling V has an engine replaced with the aid of a Coles crane mounted on a Thornycroft Amazon chassis at Lydda, Palestine. The Coles crane was an essential piece of kit for the RAF. When one was needed for the isolated airfield at Jiwani, near the border with Iran, it took 17 gruelling days for a small convoy of RAF vehicles, including the crane, to travel 1,500 miles from Karachi to Jiwani in 1945. The mountain roads were so bad that sharp corners of rock had often to be cut away to allow a passage for the vehicles.

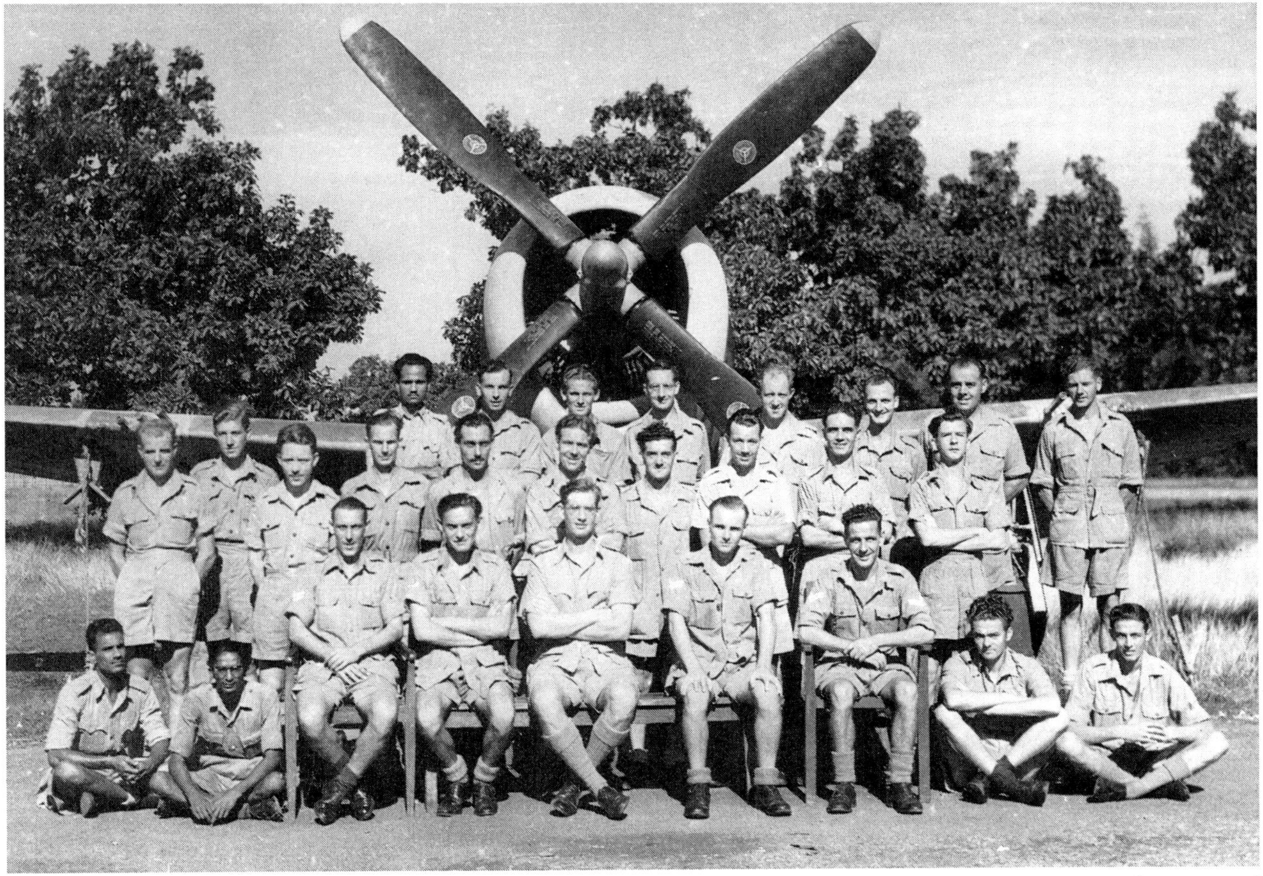

A group of RAF airmen, including three Indians, pose before a Republic P-47D Thunderbolt in south India c. 1945. All of the RAF's Thunderbolts were assigned to squadrons in South East Asia Command (India and Burma). The first Thunderbolts arrived at Drigh Road for assembly in February 1944 but in May Thunderbolt assembly was moved to Madras. After the war the British airmen in south Asia began to look forward to being demobbed but the slow rate of demobilisation became a major grievance. Declassified reports later showed that British servicemen were retained in India to control possible unrest as the Indian independence movement gained momentum. A mutiny began at RAF Drigh Road on 19th January 1946 when 1,200 airmen defied their commanding officer and refused to parade in their best blue as ordered and instead wore their customary khaki drill. The CO said the airmen's grievances would be discussed with senior officers from Air HQ in Delhi. However, the rank-and-file's act of mutiny spread like wildfire to other RAF stations in India and Ceylon and even to Singapore. The mutinies, or strikes as socialist writers and commentators preferred to call them, lasted between three and 11 days and were peaceably resolved.

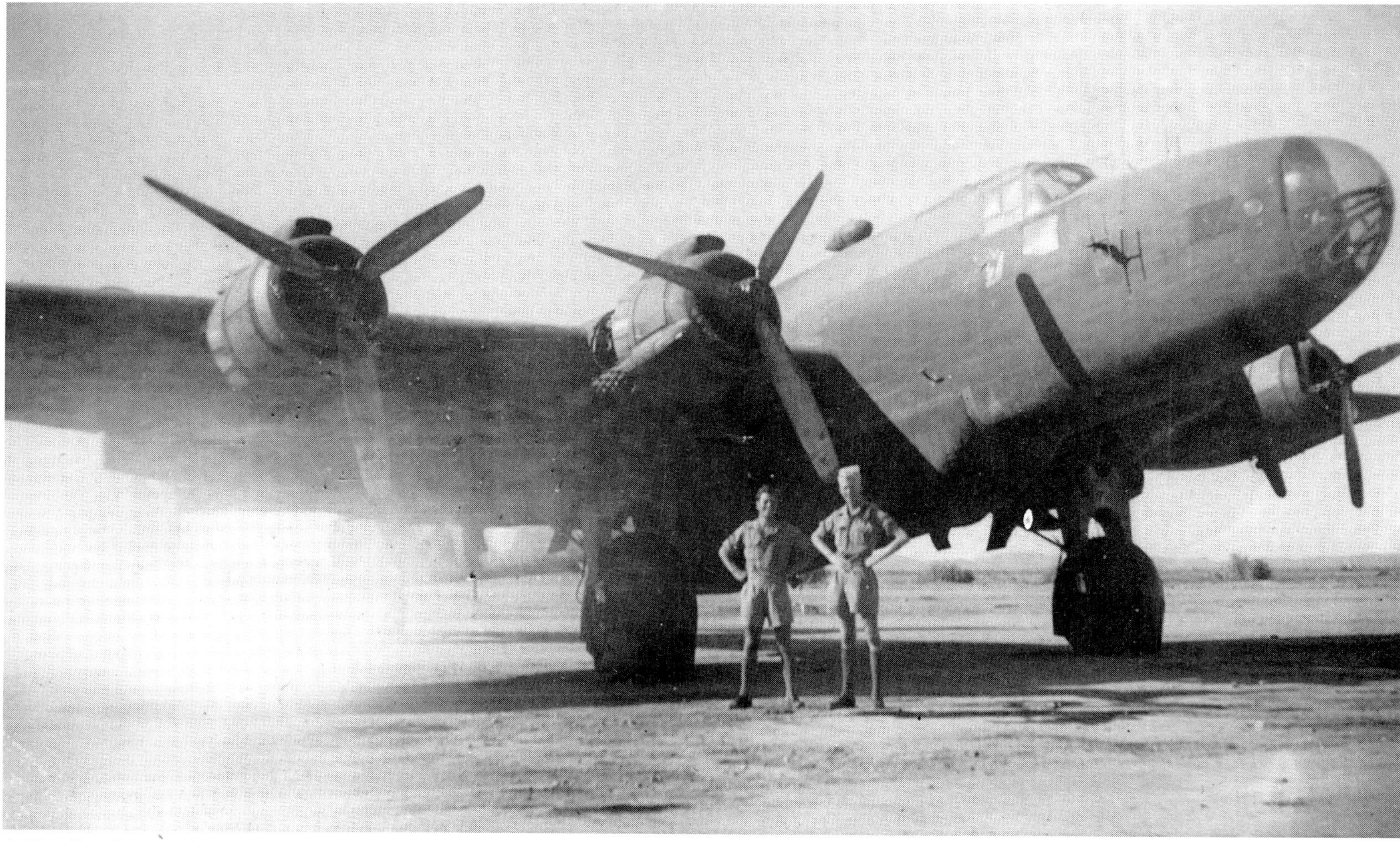

A Handley Page Halifax A. VII of No. 298 Squadron, RAF, at Mauripur in November 1946, a month before the squadron was disbanded. This unit had switched from supporting airborne forces to transport duties in September 1945, and some of its Halifaxes were used to fly the Hump run from India to China. No. 298's scheduled runs increased during October by the addition of a new route which included Nagpur, Dum Dum (Calcutta), Santa Cruz (Bombay) and Mauripur. In January 1946, two of the squadron's Halifaxes transported 100 hospital cases from Bilaspur to Mauripur at the rate of 16 a day. In March, No. 298 took part in the Operation Hunger famine-relief programme in which bags of rice were dropped from the fuselage at specified dropping zones while the bags in the freight pannier were delivered to a central location.

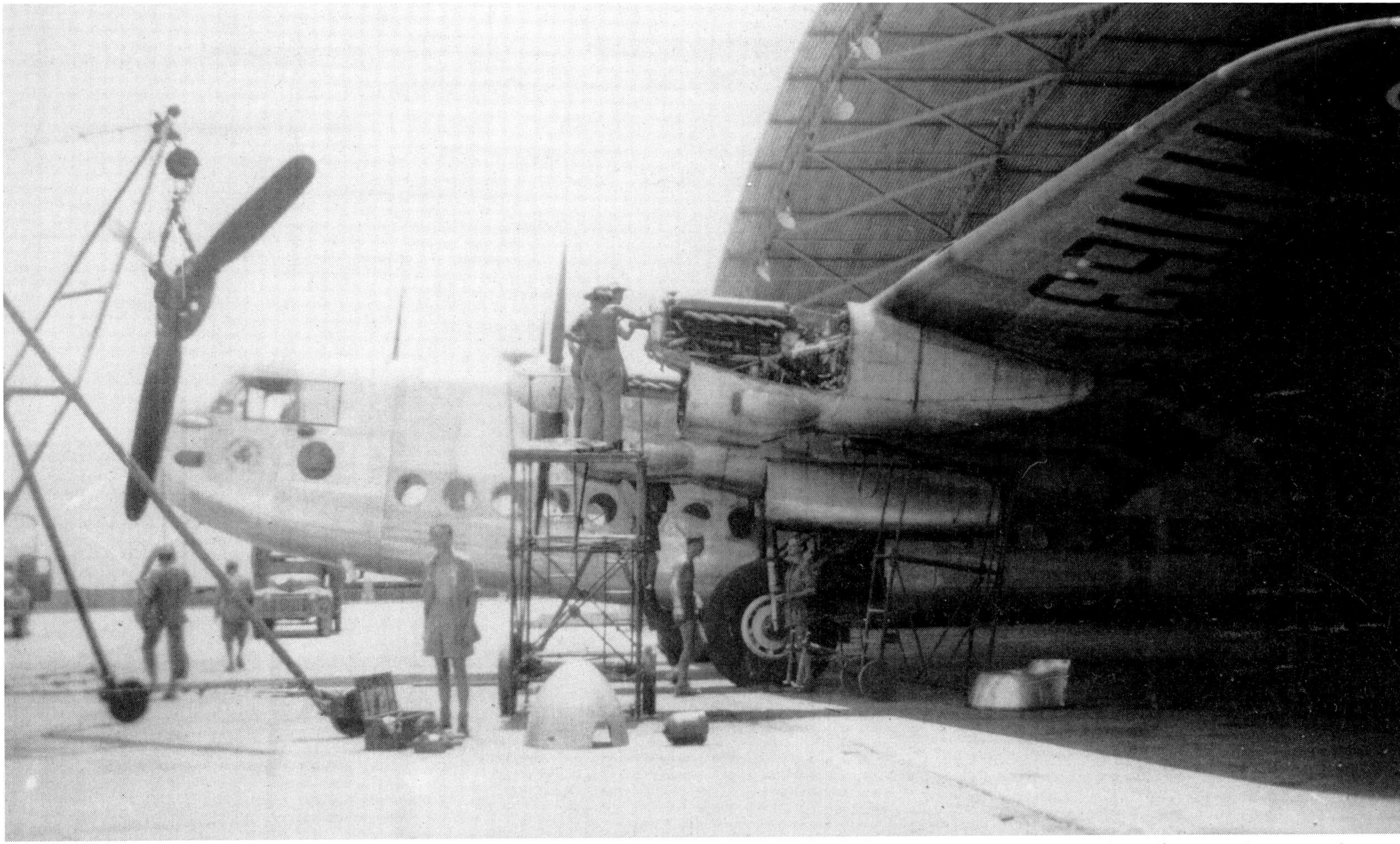

Fitters work on a Rolls-Royce Merlin engine of Avro York MW163, of No. 511 Squadron, RAF, at Mauripur, c. 1946. Yorks from this squadron were frequent visitors to Mauripur although it lost MW118 after it was damaged beyond repair while landing at the aerodrome on 8th February 1945. A York of RAF Transport Command brought New Delhi within two days of Britain in March 1944 by completing the 6,857-mile flight in 42hr 30min. It was carrying 8,000lb of urgent stores for South East Asia Command. The York followed the regular trunk route via Cairo and Karachi and encountered adverse weather and a 25mph head wind during the early stages. It cruised at just over 214mph. Stops en route absorbed just over 10 hours, the actual flying time being 31hr 54min, giving an average speed of 201.6mph.

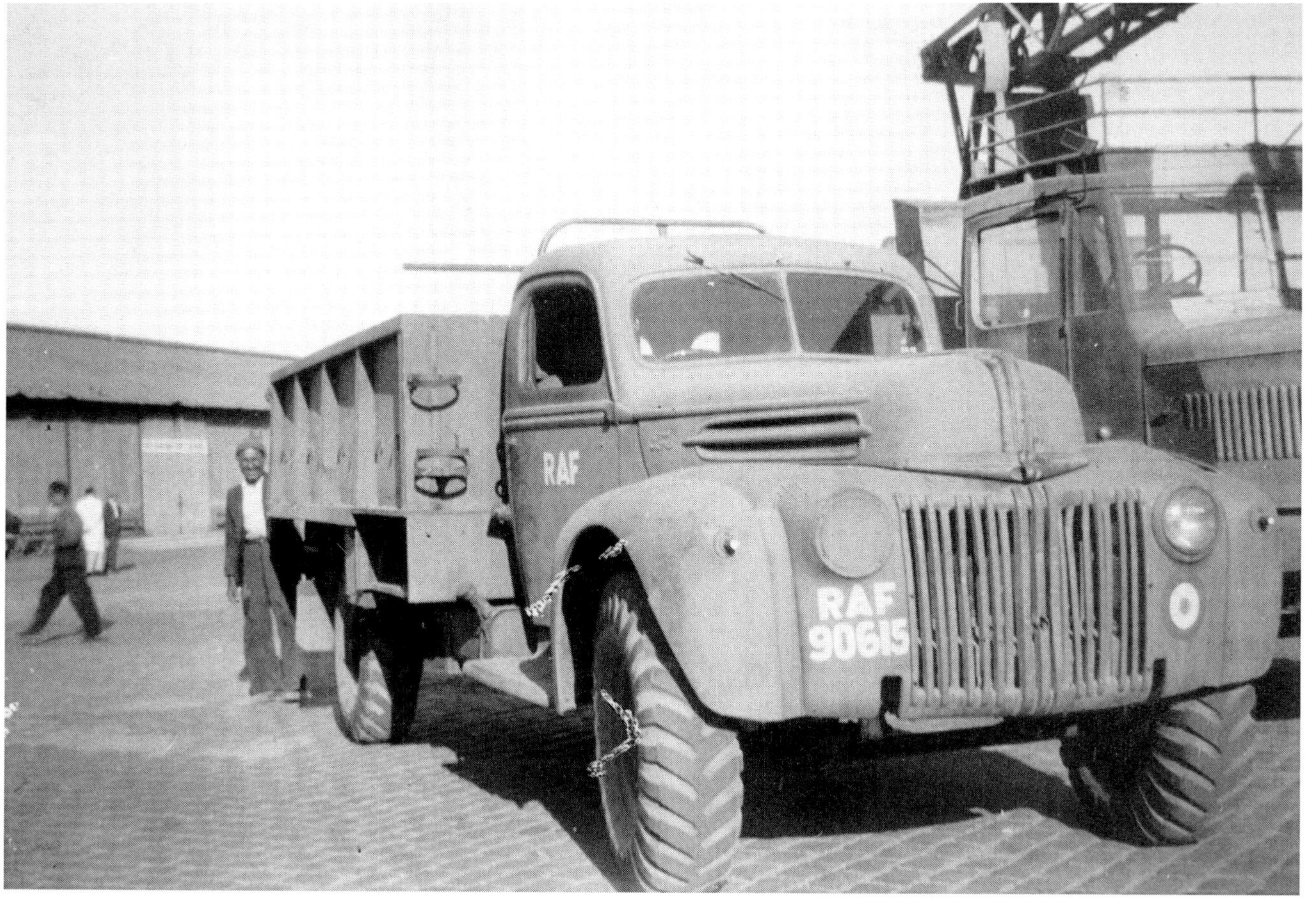

The RAF needed a sizeable transport fleet for it to function and included a variety of British and American makes, including this US-built Ford G8T lorry parked next to a Thornycroft Amazon/Coles mobile crane at an Indian seaport. Leading Aircraftman Archie Clarke, from Northamptonshire, would have helped maintain such vehicles when he was a fitter attached to the Mechanical Transport Repair Section at No. 320 Maintenance Unit, RAF Drigh Road, in 1947. He occasionally described the nature of his work in letters home. In July 1947, he wrote: "The strength has risen to about 60 in our section now. We work two weeks in the mornings and the 3rd week we don't start until afternoon. That is we start from 1 p.m. and finish at 6 o'clock. It also means that only a quarter of the strength is working at one time. If it is a turn for duty fitter instead of during the complete 24 hrs then we start after dinner or according to the shift and still get the next day off so isn't too bad at all." He goes on to mention that the section's breakdown lorry is an AEC Matador – "A big clumsy looking effort about 5 ½ tons. Anyhow they have given 12 of us licences to drive it. Some had tests but I had my licence altered to Heavy Goods."

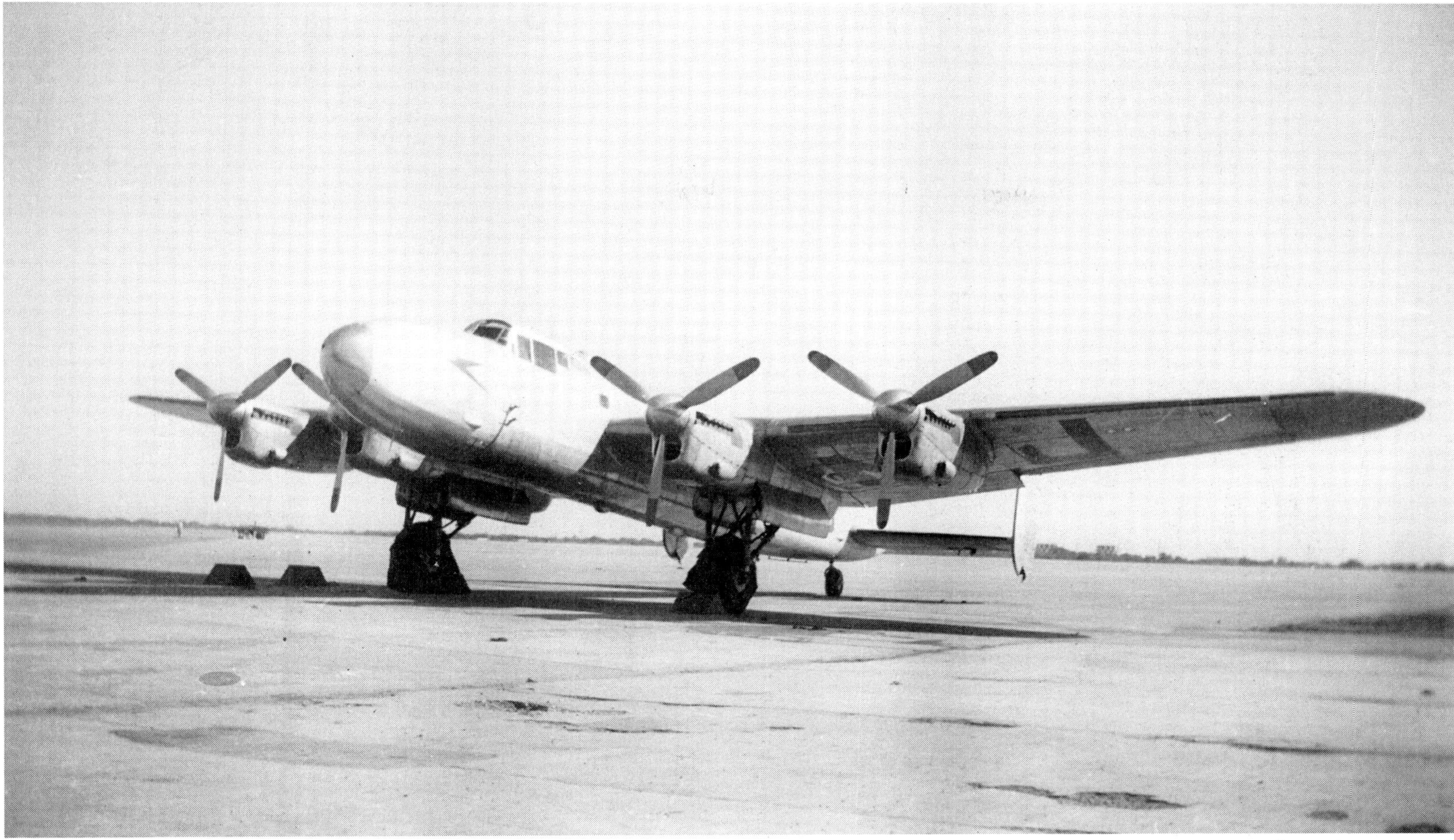

BOAC Avro Lancastrian G-AGMJ at Karachi Airport, c. 1946. It was later converted to a freighter, being named *Naseby* and was disposed of in January 1951. The airline used the Lancastrian in the early postwar years to pioneer its landplane route to Sydney. At Karachi, the BOAC crew members handed the aircraft and its passengers to Qantas Empire Airways to complete the journey to Australia. Brian Sullivan, who flew as a junior cabin steward with BOAC, recalled in *Aeroplane Monthly* (July 1995) flying in the airline's Lancastrians from Heathrow to Karachi in 1946. He said that once while flying the sector from Lydda to Karachi, he woke from a snooze to find that all the flight crew were fast asleep: "The aircraft, with only the autopilot to control it, was flying quietly on into the desert night, presumably well on its way towards the southern extremities of Russia". He roused the radio officer who stirred the other crew members. They eventually got the airliner back on course although fortunately the sleeping passengers were unaware of this drama.

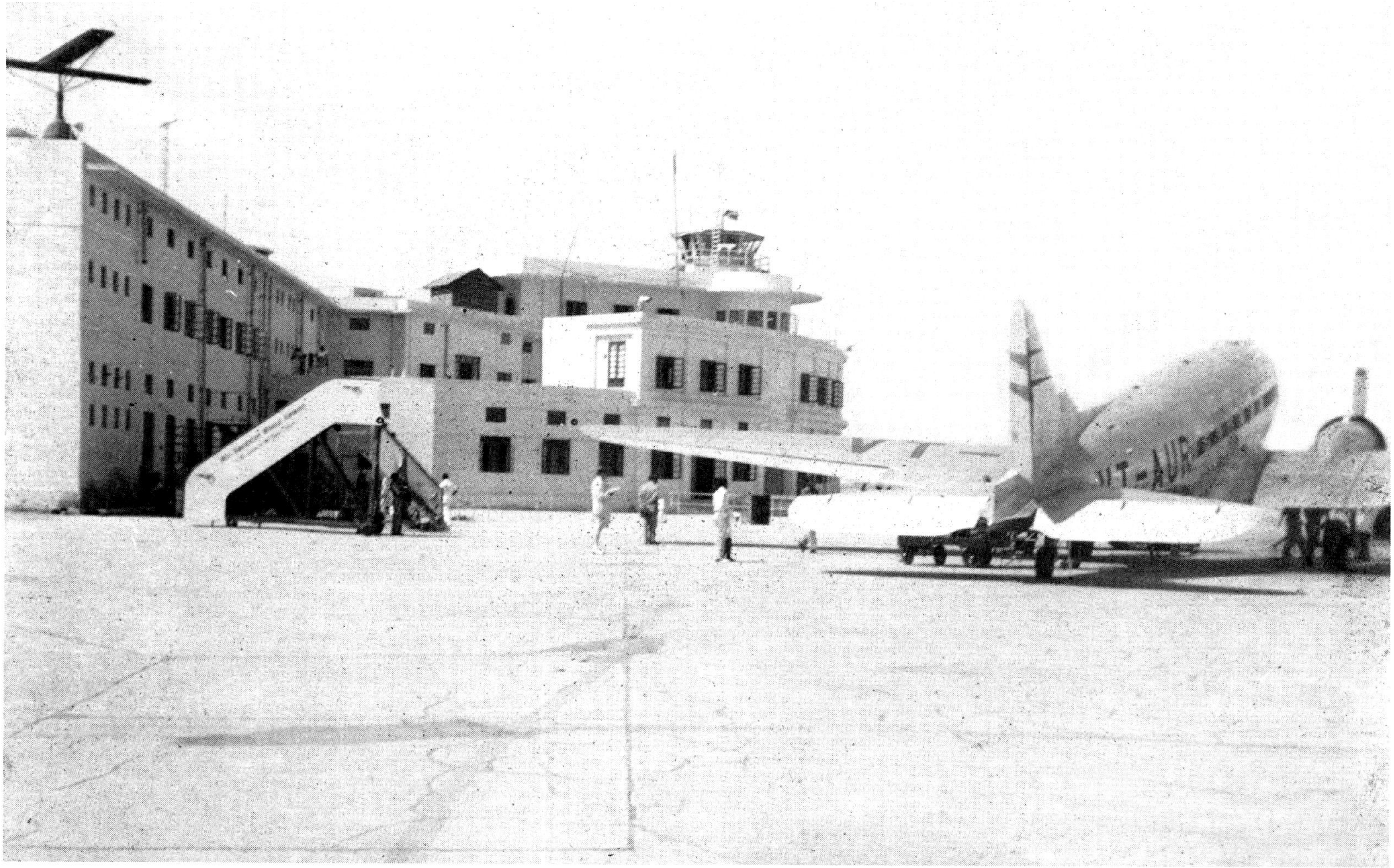

Air-India's Douglas C-47 Dakota VT-AUR at Karachi Airport, c. 1946. The handsome appearance of the control tower and terminal building symbolise Karachi's status as one of the leading airports in south Asia at that time. Air-India was the successor in July 1946 to Tata Air Lines, which was founded by J.R.D. Tata who had made the first mail flight in October 1932 between Karachi, Ahmedabad and Bombay, while his business partner, Nevill Vintcent, flew the last sector from Bellary to Madras.

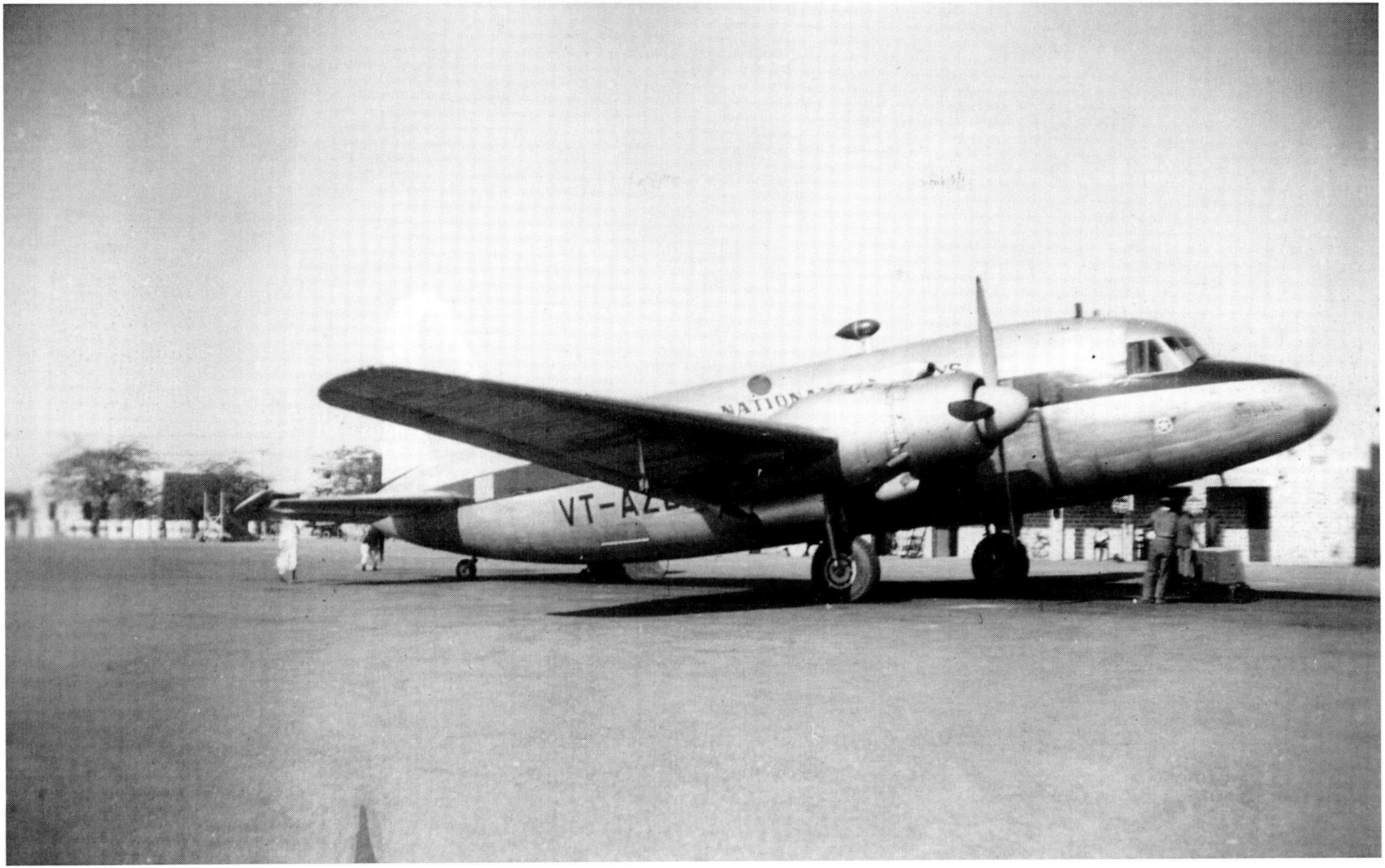

Vickers Viking 1B VT-AZB of Indian National Airways at Jodhpur Airport, c. 1947. Jodphur was a staging post on the daily Delhi-Karachi service which was inaugurated on 1st January 1946. INA also introduced a thrice weekly service between Delhi, Lahore, Chaklala and Peshawar. Variants of the Douglas Dakota were used initially on these routes. Viking VT-AZB was delivered to INA on 28th October 1946 and was one of six of the type bought by the operator between 1946 and 1948 and later inherited by Indian Airlines Corporation in 1953.

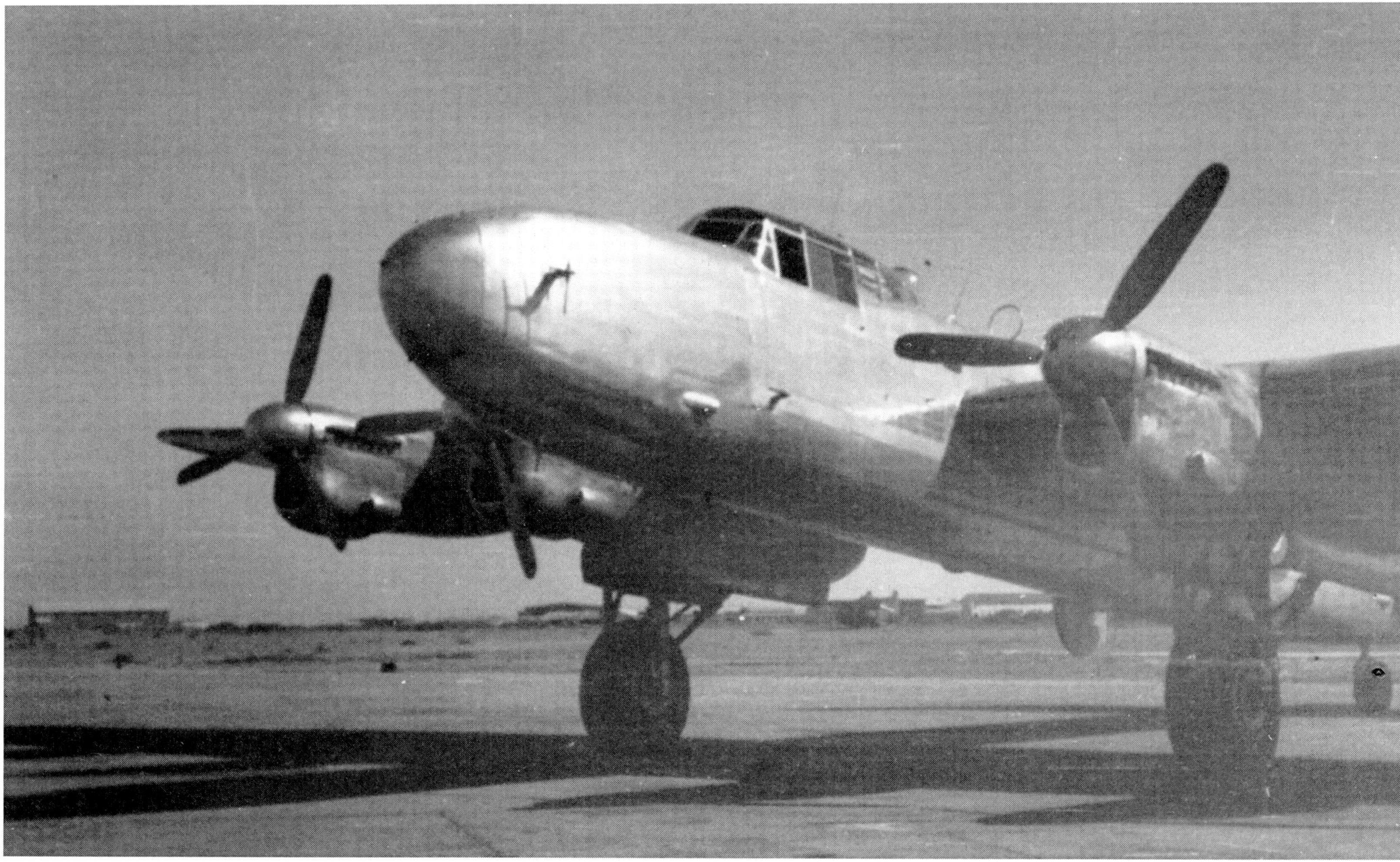

A VIP Avro Lancastrian at RAF Mauripur in January 1947. Similar Lancastrian PD328 *Aries* of the RAF's Empire Air Navigation School also visited Mauripur and was in the headlines for some of its record-breaking long-distance flights after the war, including England to Cape Town in 32hr 21min in January 1946. It also made flights over the geographical and magnetic North poles in May 1946. During its penultimate flight before being retired, *Aries* broke the London-Karachi, London-Darwin and London-Wellington FAI (Fédération Aéronautique Internationale) records in the outward journey of a liaison mission to Australasia in 1946.

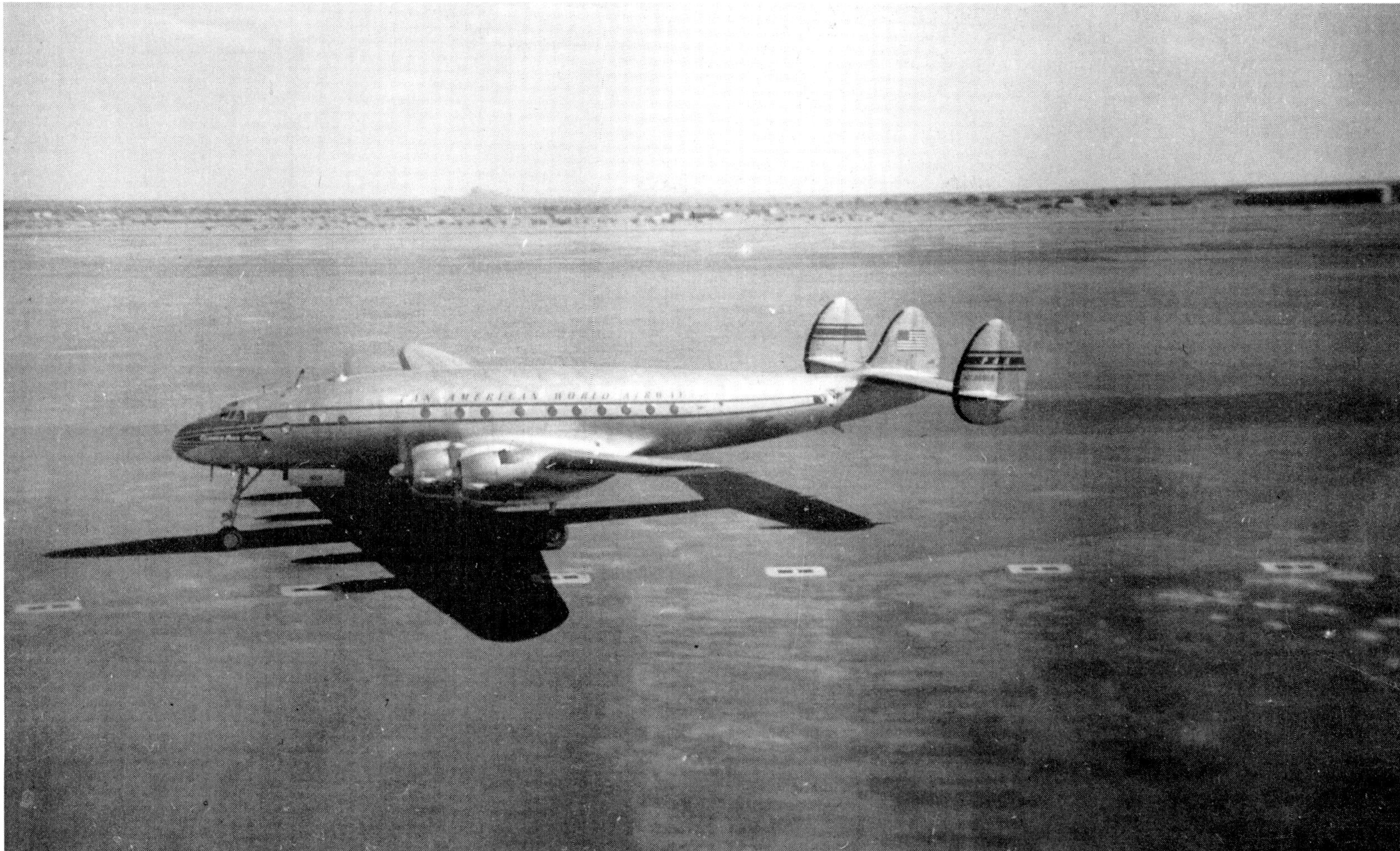

Lockheed L-049 Constellation NC 88833 *Clipper Bald Eagle* of Pan American World Airways at Karachi Airport, c. 1947. The airline had introduced the Constellation on its first Clipper air mail flight to India, departing from New York on 7th March 1947 and arriving at Karachi on 10th March. Three months later, PAA inaugurated the first scheduled round-the-world air service. A Constellation flew the sector from New York to Calcutta via Gander, Shannon, Heathrow, Istanbul and Karachi. At Calcutta it met Pan Am's Douglas DC-4 Skymaster flight from San Francisco. In 1948 a PAA Constellation departed Heathrow for Calcutta on Saturdays at 2.05pm; the return flight arriving back from India at 7.55pm on Wednesdays.

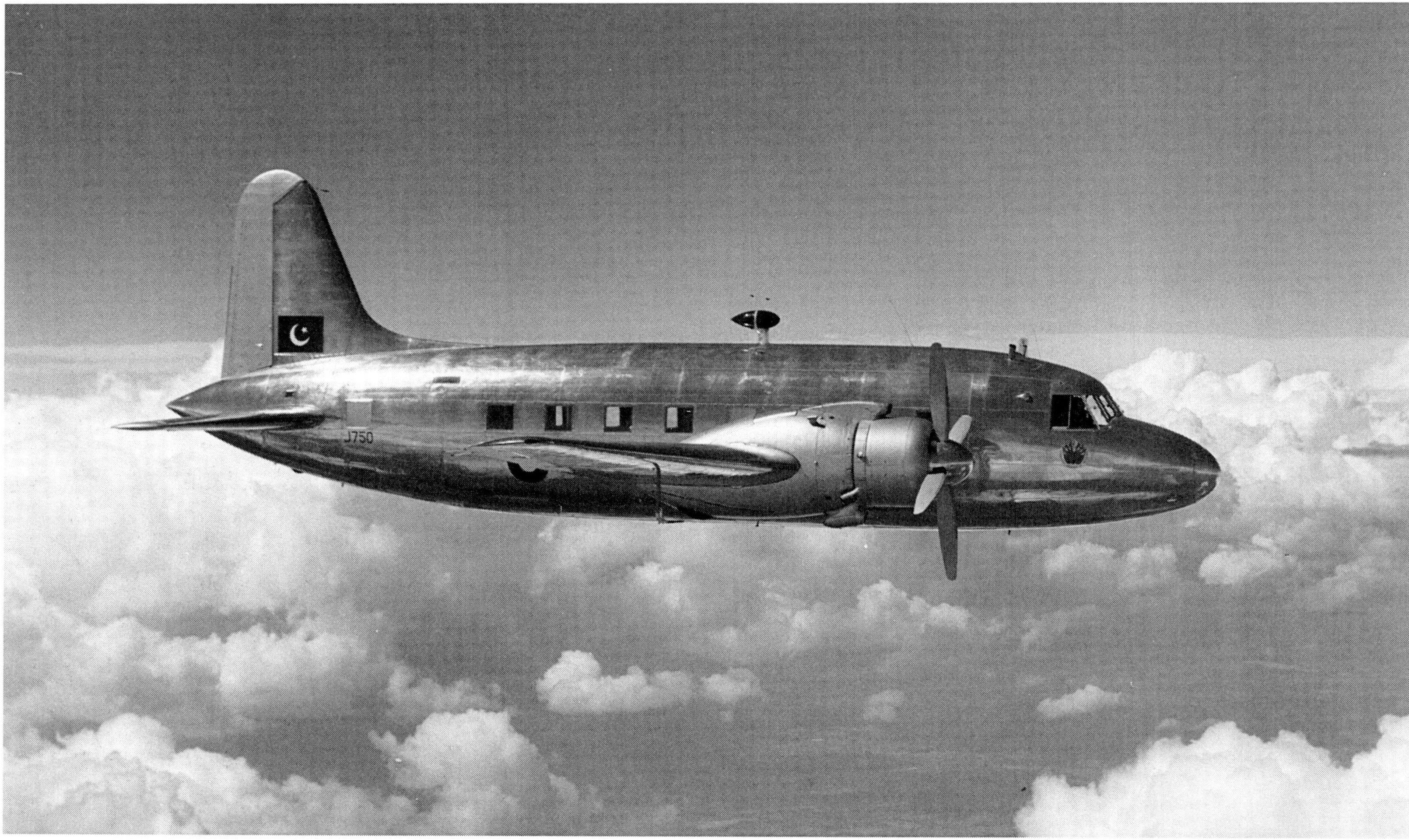

Charles E. Brown photographed Vickers Viking 1B J750 of the Royal Pakistan Air Force probably before it was delivered to the RPAF on 14th June 1948. This VIP transport was used briefly by Mohammad Ali Jinnah, the founder of Pakistan and the dominion's first governor-general, before his death on 11th September 1948. In 1956, a Vickers Viscount replaced J750 which was withdrawn from use and stored at PAF Peshawar. It has since become one of the star exhibits at the Pakistan Air Force Museum at PAF Faisal, formerly RAF Drigh Road. The Viking was carefully disassembled at Peshawar and transported the 1,000 miles to Karachi on lowloaders. After it was reassembled, great care was needed to ease it past various obstacles such as walls, telegraph poles and guardrooms before placing the Viking in an RAF-era hangar which forms part of the museum in the south-west corner of the base.

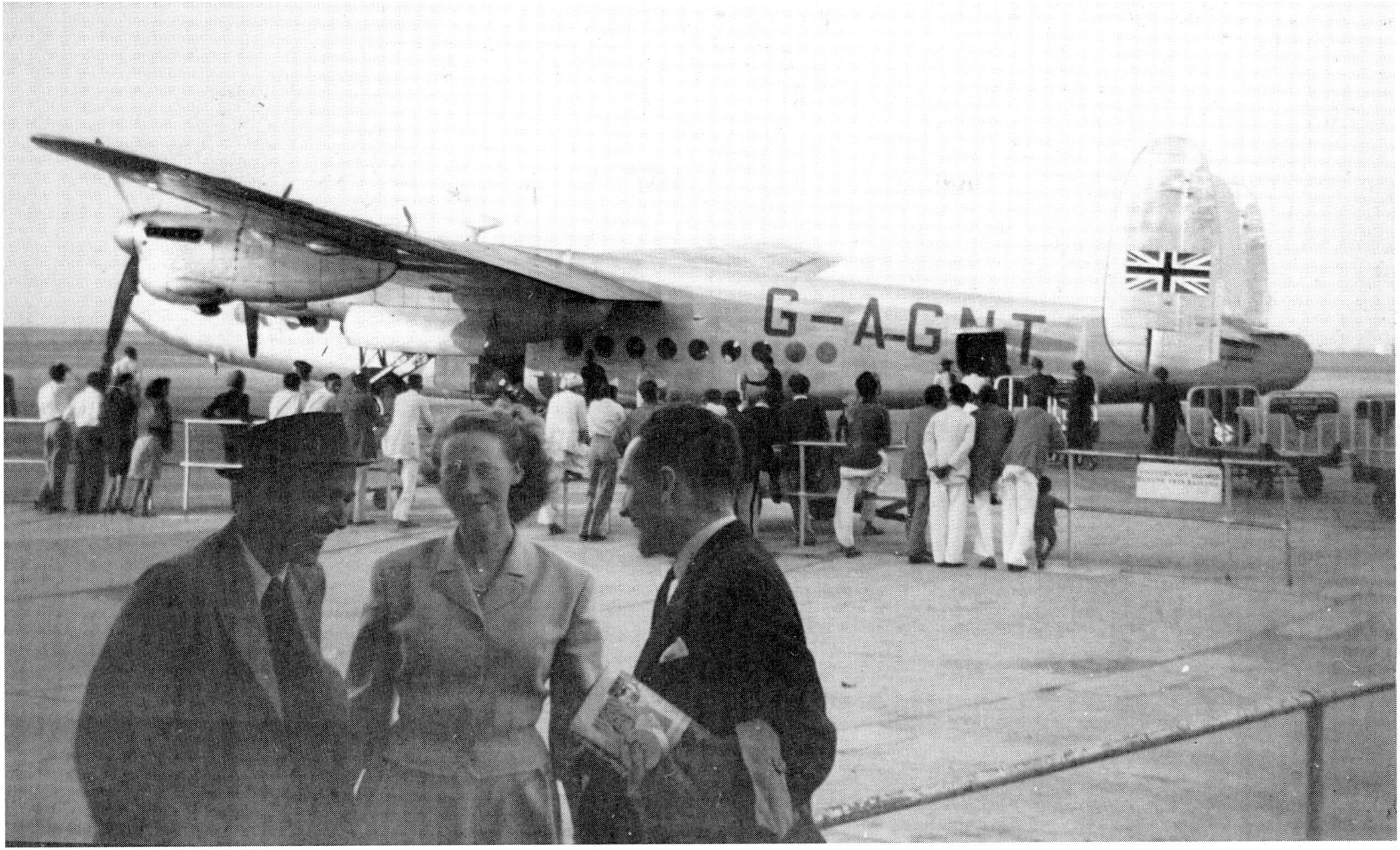

A busy scene on the apron at Karachi Airport as BOAC Avro York G-AGNT is prepared for departure to Calcutta on 5th December 1948. Earlier that year, the airline's Yorks had begun flying three times a week from London to Calcutta and one service a week to Karachi and Delhi. Following the partition of India in August 1947, BOAC responded to an appeal from the Pakistan government and made Avro York G-AGJA, one Lancastrian and nine Dakotas available to help fly 7,000 people from Delhi to Karachi. Ten further Dakotas from British independent operators also participated in the air evacuation. The first arrival at Karachi was on 31st August and the operation concluded on 17th September.

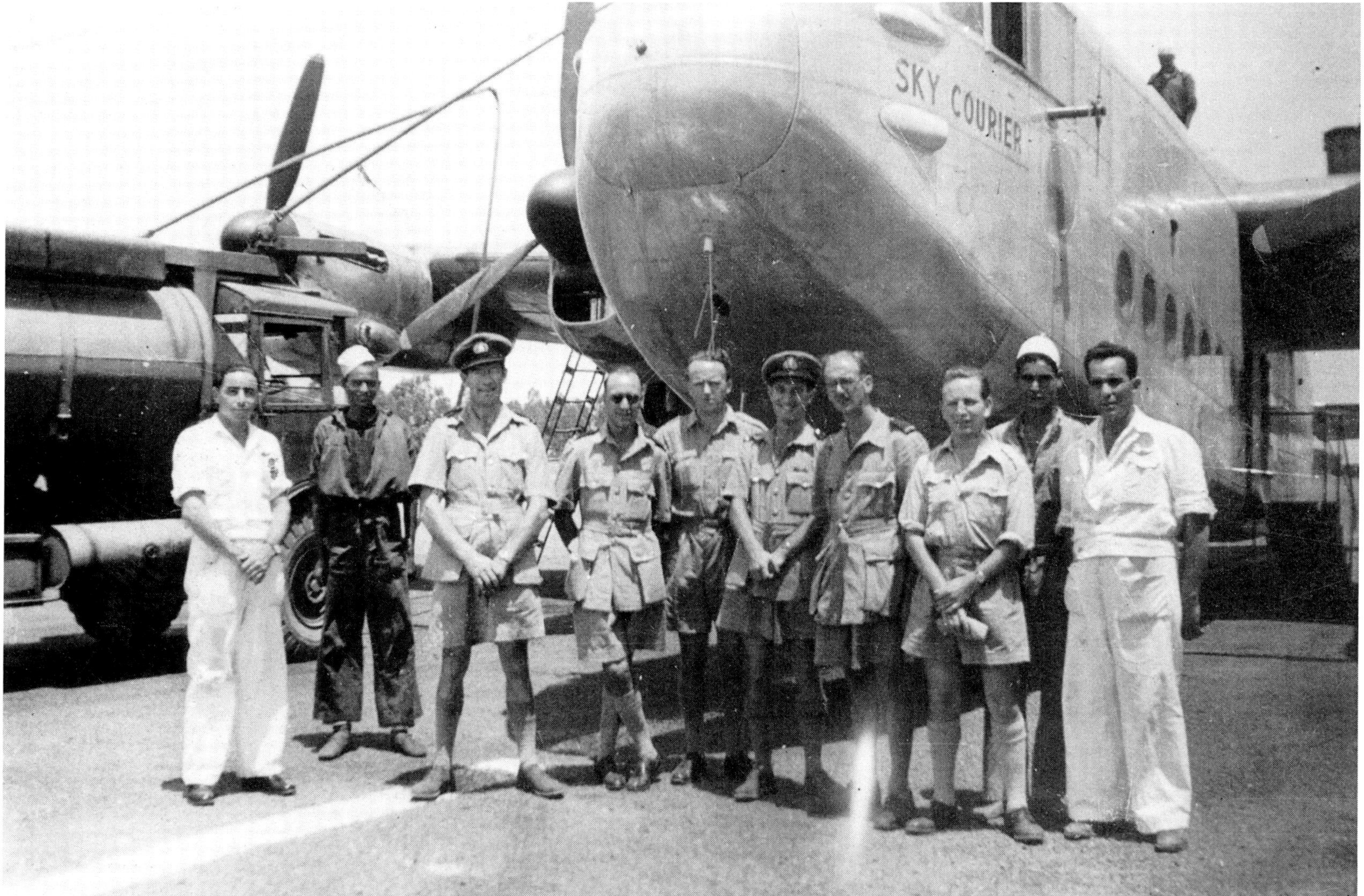

The crew of Skyways' Avro York G-AHLV pose with ground staff at Basra, Iraq, in 1948. The airline operated a twice-weekly service from the UK to Basra while under contract to the Anglo-Iranian Oil Co, and its Yorks also flew services to Karachi on behalf of BOAC, which began on 3rd August 1946.

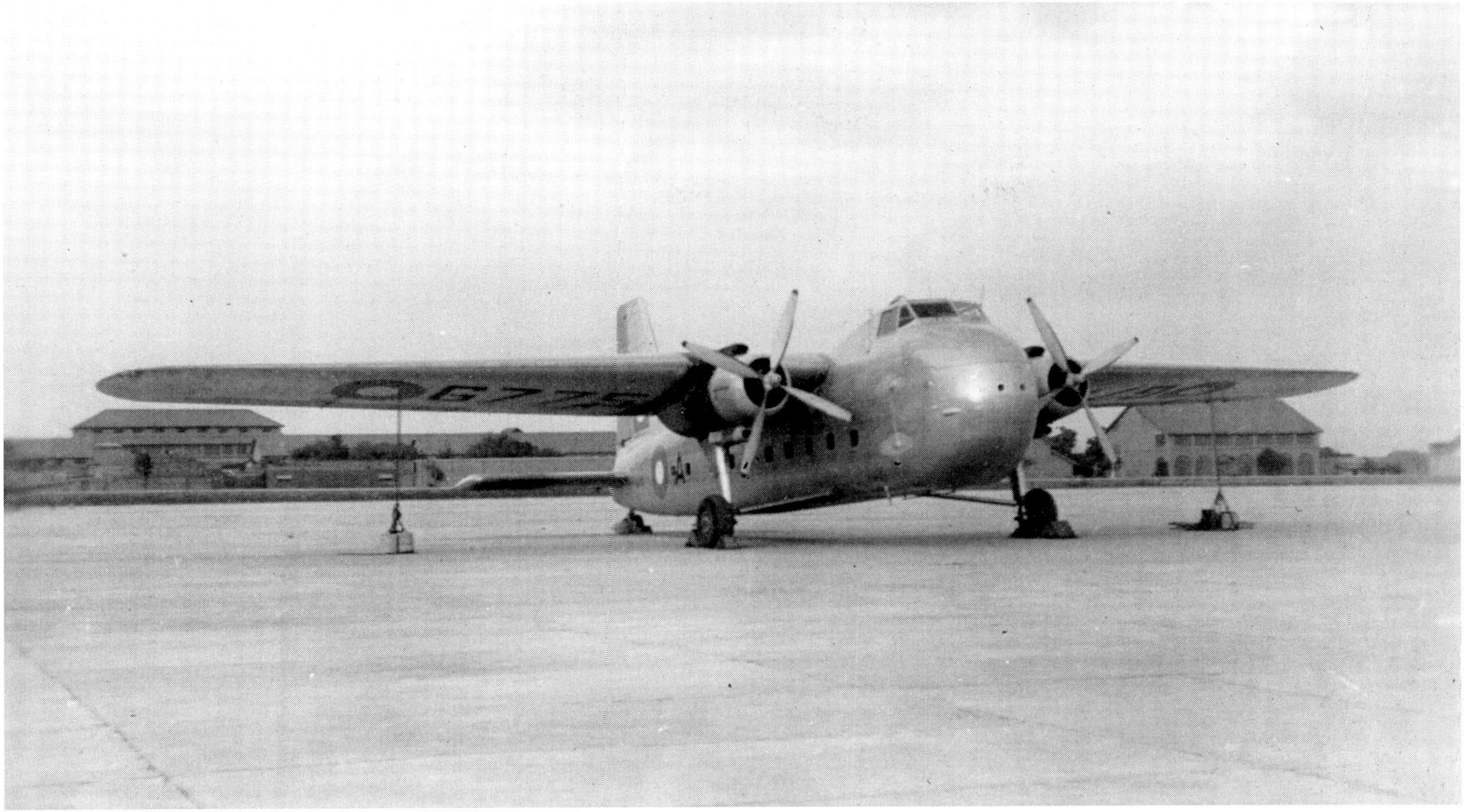

Bristol 170 Freighter Mk. 21E G775 of the Royal Pakistan Air Force at Mauripur in 1949. It was delivered on 15th August 1948 and was the first of 81 Bristol 170s which saw service with the RPAF/PAF until the late-1960s. G775 survived until 21st August 1969 when it was damaged beyond repair. Pakistan was persuaded to buy the Bristol 170 instead of the twin-engined Bristol 164 Brigand light ground-attack bomber. Two Brigands were evaluated by the RPAF in 1948 of which one crashed and the other was returned to the RAF. It has been alleged that the British thought the Brigand was too much of a "hot ship" for the Pakistanis to handle and so the rather sedate Freighter was offered instead. The former colonial power was being rather disingenuous when it was claimed that the Bristol 170 could be modified to become a bomber. Former Pakistan Air Force pilot Mansoor Shah, in his book *The Gold Bird*, said the Freighter's crews, during operational training, "found it extremely difficult to get their practice bombs anywhere near the outer circle. Ultimately, we also discovered that the weight of the bombs on the undercarriage caused undue stress. This resulted in cracks developing in the gear assembly".

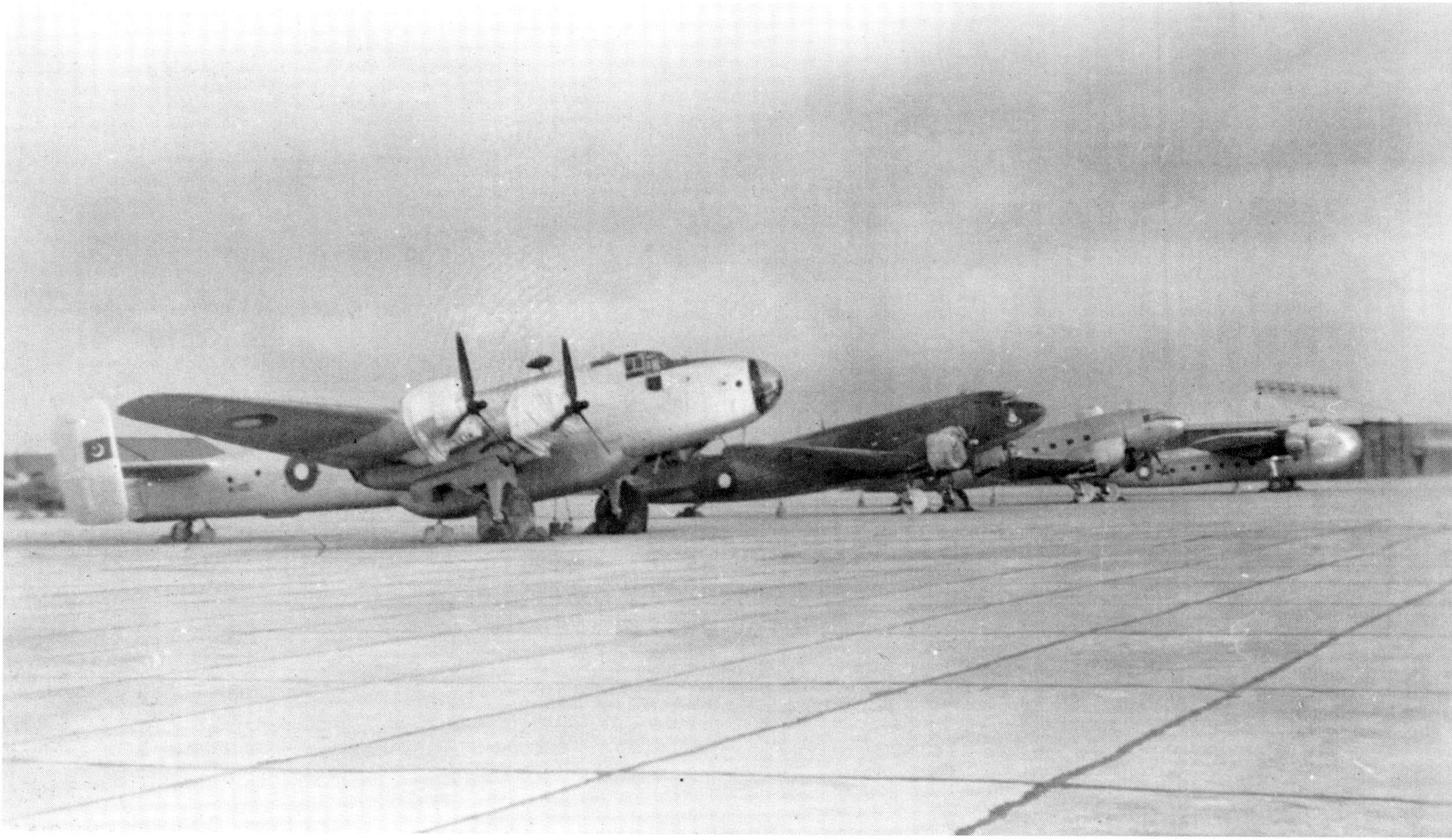

A Royal Pakistan Air Force line-up of a Handley Page Halifax, two Douglas C-47 Dakotas and a Bristol 170 Freighter at Mauripur in 1949. The RPAF bought eight Halifax B.VIs to form a bomber squadron and they were flown from Stansted to Thame airfield for overhaul by Airtech Ltd. The aircraft were ferried out by British American Air Services' crews to Pakistan in October 1949 and on arrival at Mauripur they formed No. 12 Squadron, RPAF. In service, the Halifaxes were stripped of their former wartime camouflage and operated in bare metal finish, as seen in the photo, on reconnaissance and transport duties. Three civilianised Halifax C.VIIIs were bought to supplement the fleet and were ferried to Pakistan in May 1948. One force-landed north-west of Shaibah because of a lack of fuel and was damaged beyond repair. The two survivors were flown by Pak-Air Ltd and ended their days as instructional airframes until the Halifax B.VIs were withdrawn in 1955.

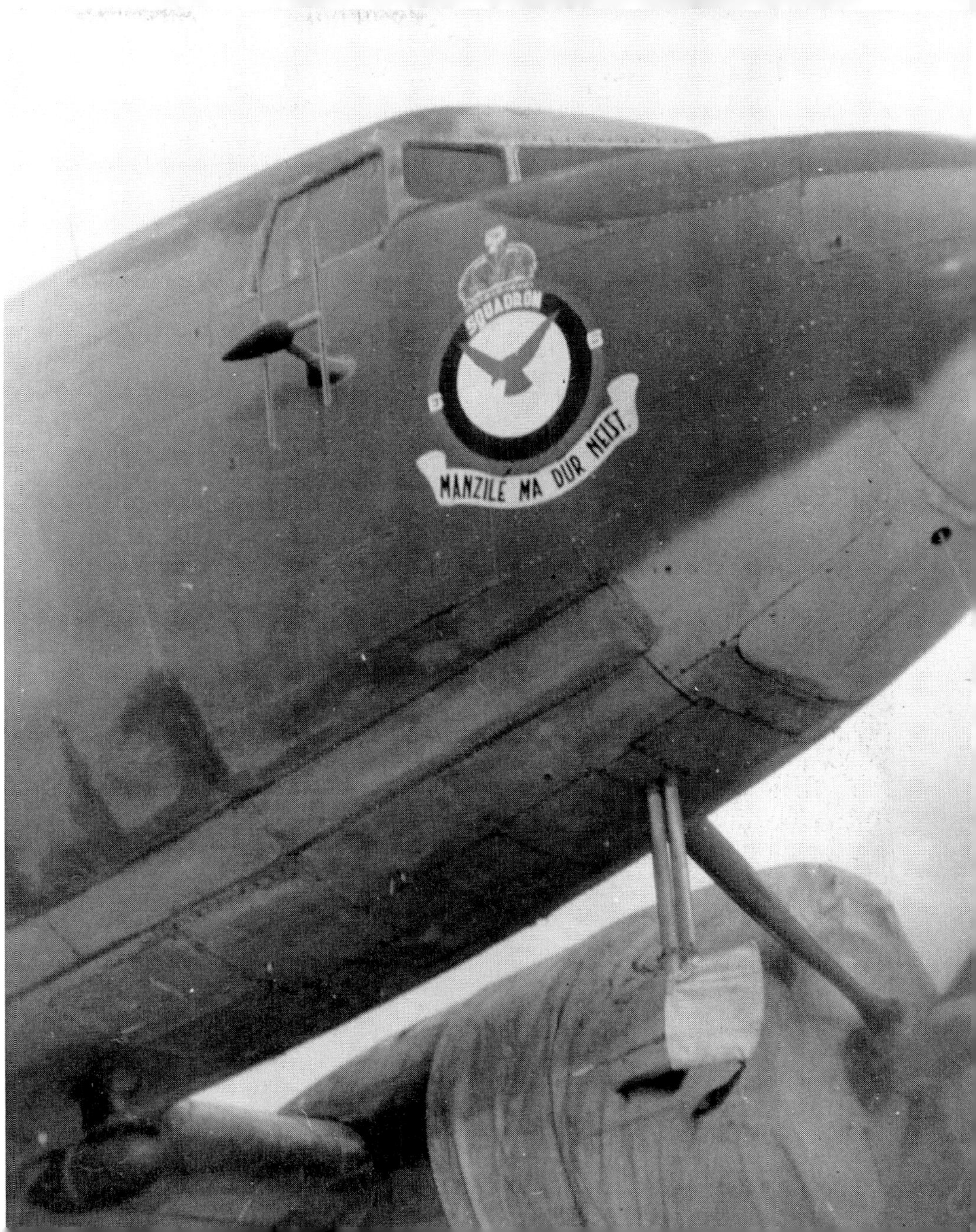

A Dakota of No. 6 Squadron, Royal Pakistan Air Force, whose squadron crest is displayed prominently. The motto, *Manzile na dur meist*, translates as No destination is out of my reach.

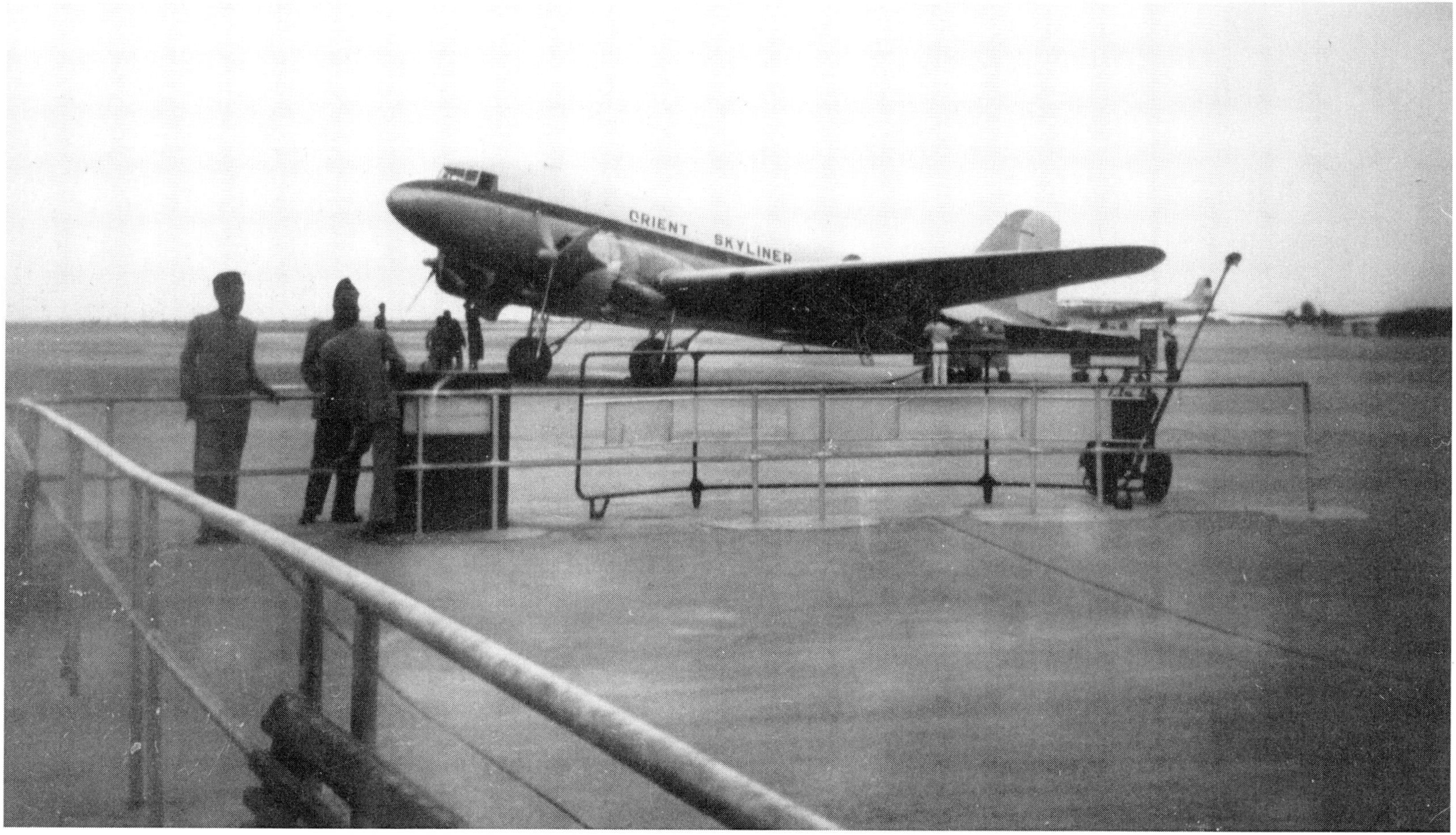

A Douglas DC-3 Dakota of Orient Airways waits to depart from Karachi to Lahore on 14th August 1952. Orient Airways was Pakistan's first indigenous airline although it had been established originally in Calcutta on 23rd October 1946 by Mirza Ahmad Ispahani, who was a leading industrialist. He received the backing of Pakistan's founding father, Mohammad Ali Jinnah, who saw that an airline would be needed to link West and East Pakistan after independence. Four Douglas DC-3s were bought in February 1947 and operations started on 4th June that year. Orient's DC-3s played their part in assisting with the mass migration of people from India to Pakistan in the turbulent and bloody aftermath of India's partition. Orient moved its base from Calcutta to Karachi and launched scheduled services between Karachi and Dacca, via Delhi and Calcutta, and the domestic routes of Karachi-Lahore-Peshawar and Karachi-Quetta-Lahore. By 1949 Orient had a fleet of 10 DC-3s and three 40-seat Convair 240s.

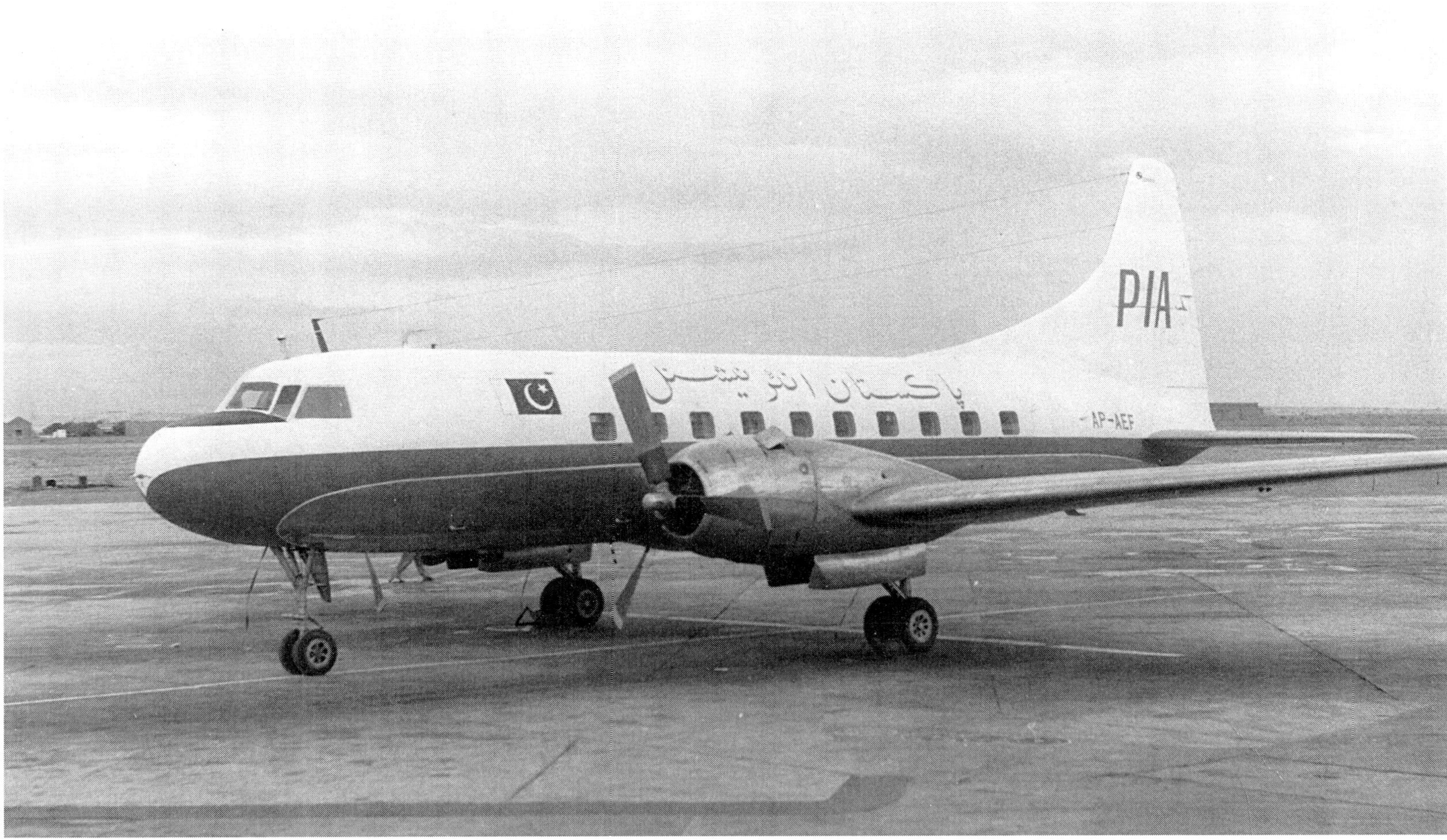

AP-AEF was one of three Convair 240s delivered to Orient Airways in 1949 and later managed by Pakistan International Airlines from 11th March 1955. They were joined in 1956 by two 240s bought from Trans Australia Airlines and flew domestic and regional routes including Karachi-Lahore, Karachi-Bombay and Lahore-Delhi. They also flew between Karachi-Lahore-Delhi-Dacca which included a stopover in the Indian capital. Two Convairs were lost in crashes in India and the remaining three were sold in 1959 to Fokker in part-exchange for PIA's first batch of Fokker F-27 Friendship turboprop airliners.

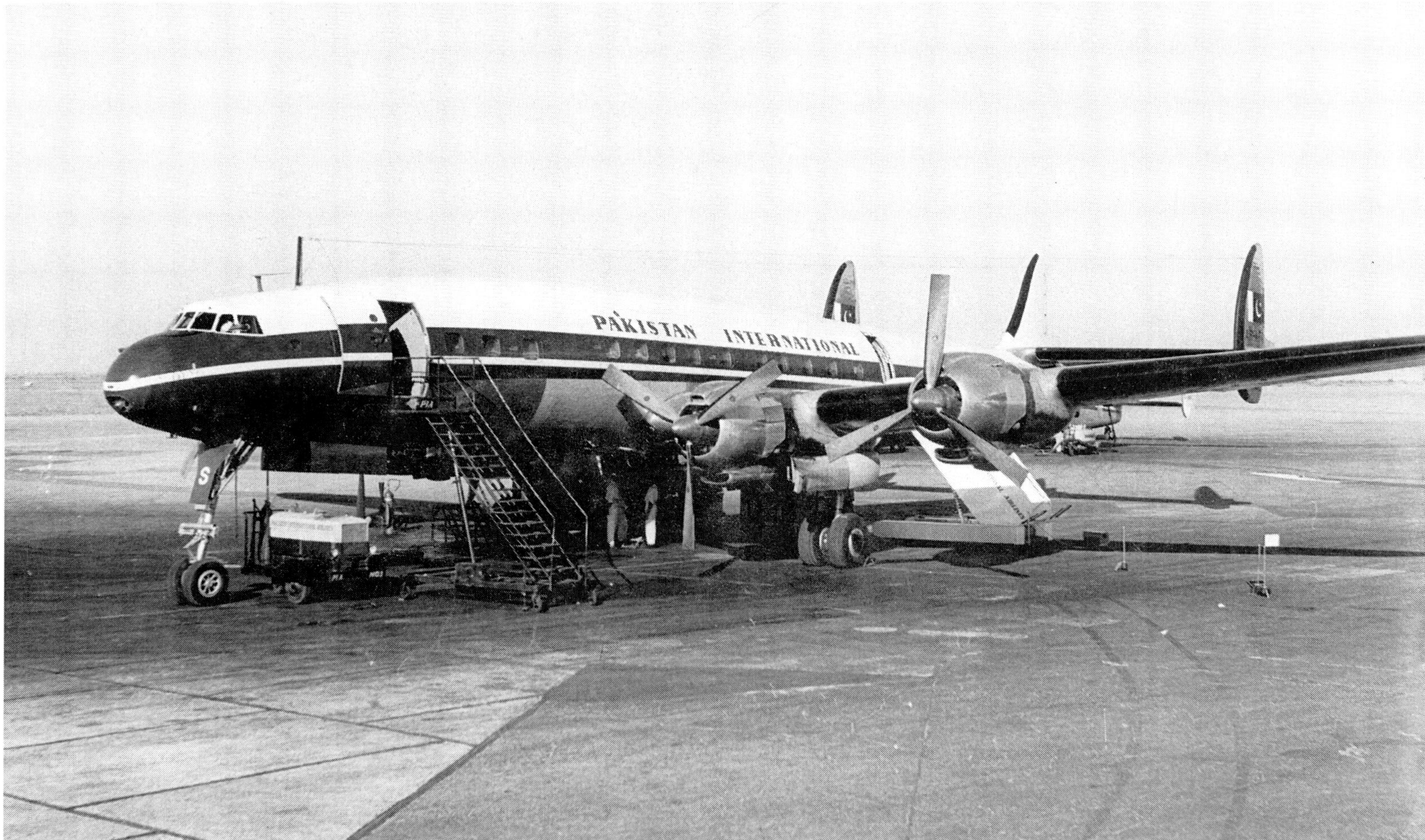

Pakistan International Airlines' Lockheed L-1049C Super Constellation AP-AFS at Karachi Airport where it is receiving attention from the airline's ground staff. AP-AFS was delivered to the Pakistan Government on 9th April 1954 and then leased to PIA before being bought by the operator in 1958. PIA's first service with its three L-1049Cs took place on 7th June 1954 between Dacca and Karachi. An international service was inaugurated on 1st February 1955 on a Karachi-Cairo-London route, with the fastest schedule so far between the two cities of 19 hours' elapsed time. The pre-inaugural flight from Karachi arrived at Heathrow on 20th January and among those on board were the Prime Minister of Pakistan, Mohammed Ali Bogra and his wife, Begum Mohammed Ali. The flight-deck crew included three Australians, two British and two Pakistanis – First Officer D. David and Radio Officer N.Y. Butt.

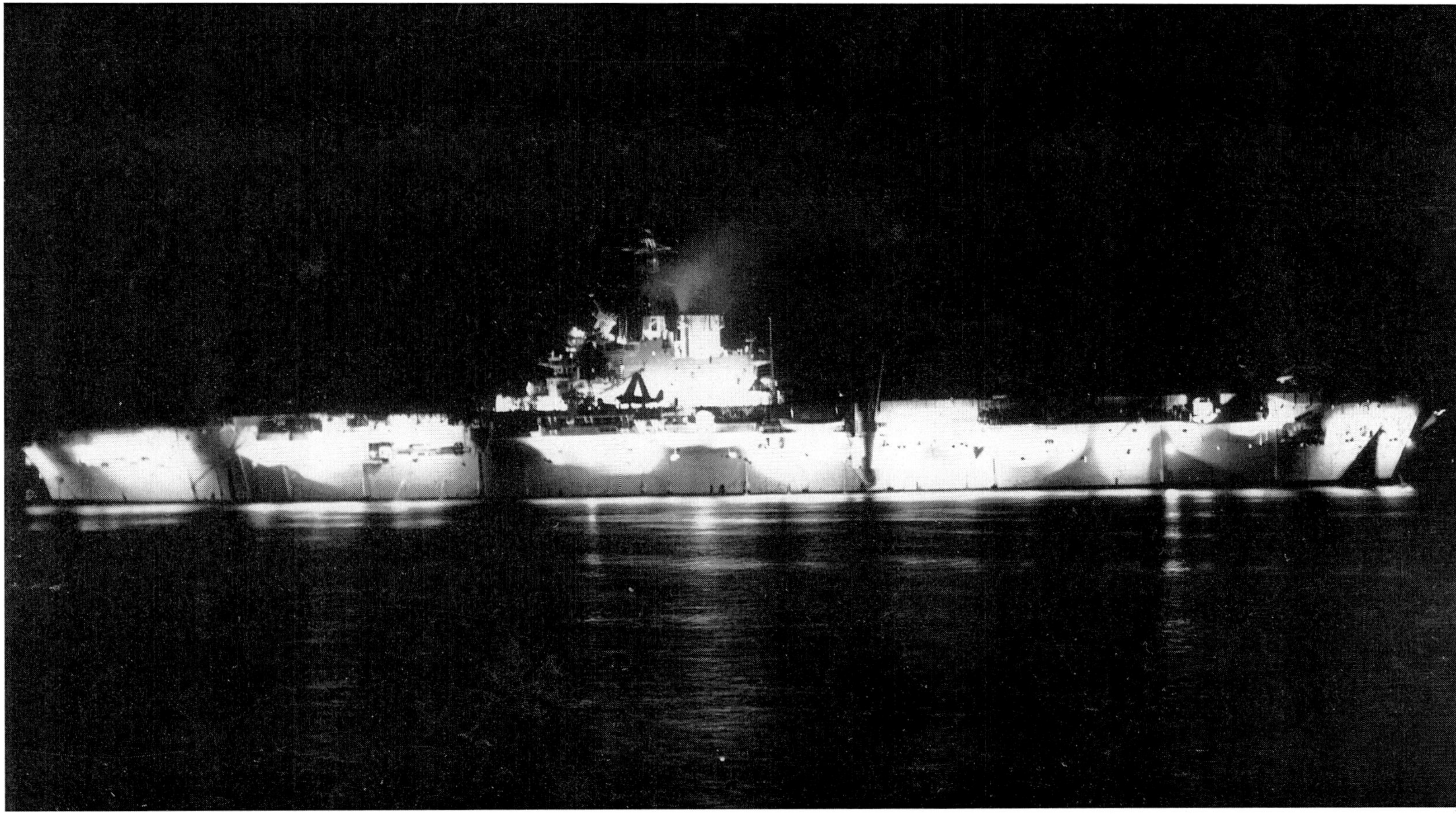

The Royal Navy's HMS *Centaur* at Karachi in February 1956 when she called at the port during a voyage to the Far East with HMS *Albion*. An aircraft carrier is always an impressive warship with which to show the flag and here *Centaur* is floodlit with one of her Hawker Sea Hawks silhouetted against her island superstructure. A crew member wrote on a postcard from Karachi to an aunt in Yorkshire that he was on his way to Singapore "on a 'Show the Flag' cruise and enjoying it very much. Cocktails at the Palace with the Governor-General tonight. Temperature is 84F and getting hotter. It will be pleasant to have cool weather on my return for Easter". Pakistan was a dominion then but not for much longer as the country was proclaimed an Islamic Republic on 23rd March 1956 with Major-General Iskander Mirza, the last governor-general, becoming Pakistan's first president. *Centaur*'s aircraft complement at the time included nine Sea Hawks of No. 803 Squadron and six Fairey Gannet AS.4s of No. 820 Squadron, Fleet Air Arm. The *Centaur* was broken up at Cairnryan, Wigtownshire, in 1972-73.

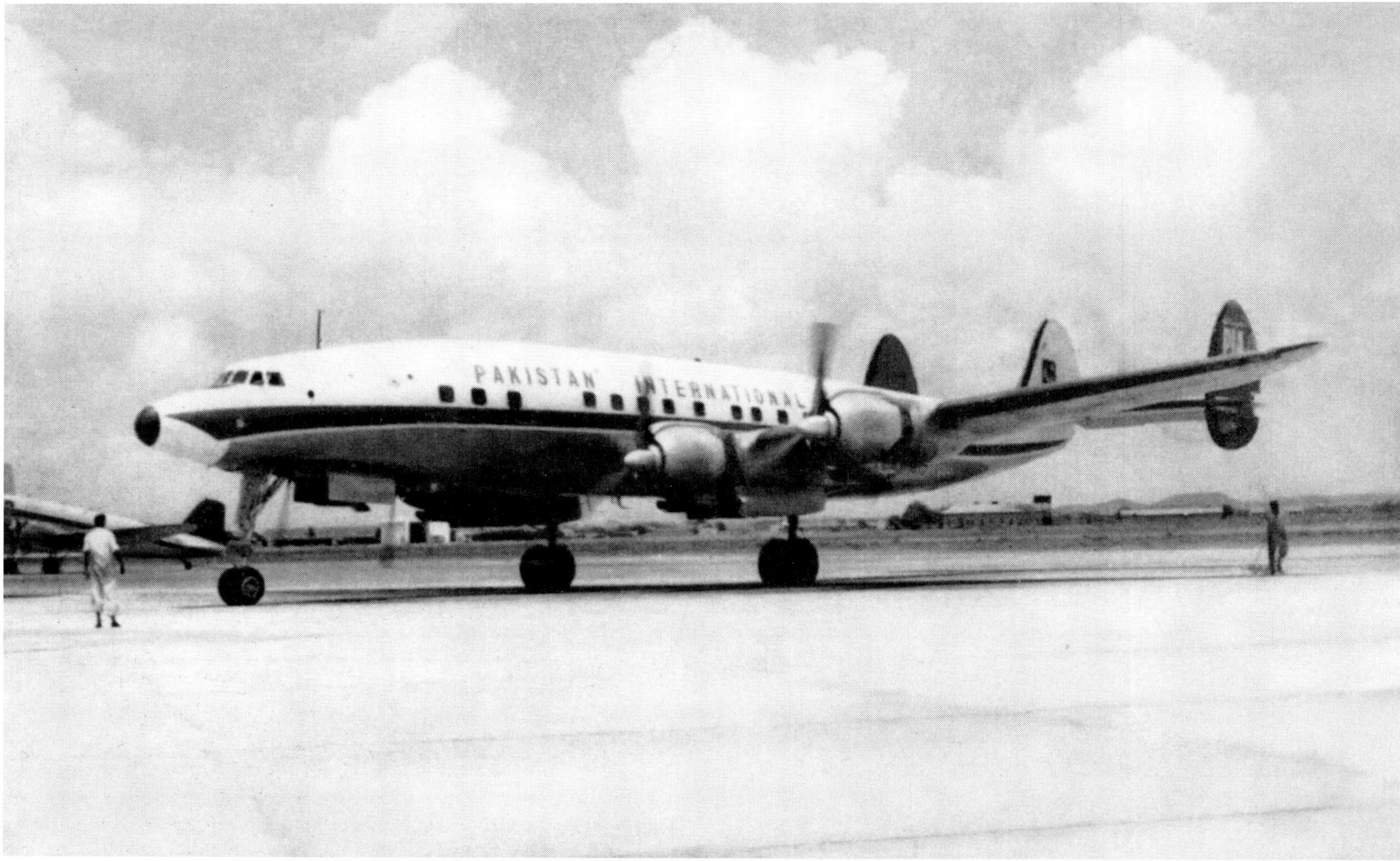

One of Pakistan International Airlines' two Lockheed L-1049H Super Constellations runs up its four 3,400hp Wright Turbo Compound piston engines at Karachi Airport. AP-AJY was delivered on 11th February 1958 while AP-AJZ followed on 3rd March. PIA had become a national corporation on 11th March 1955 when it took over the services, equipment and personnel of Orient Airways, whose shareholders received 40% of PIA's stock. M.A. Ispahani, Orient's founder, was chairman of the new corporation, which became responsible for the operation of all air services within West and East Pakistan and regional services to Bombay, Delhi, Calcutta and Rangoon.

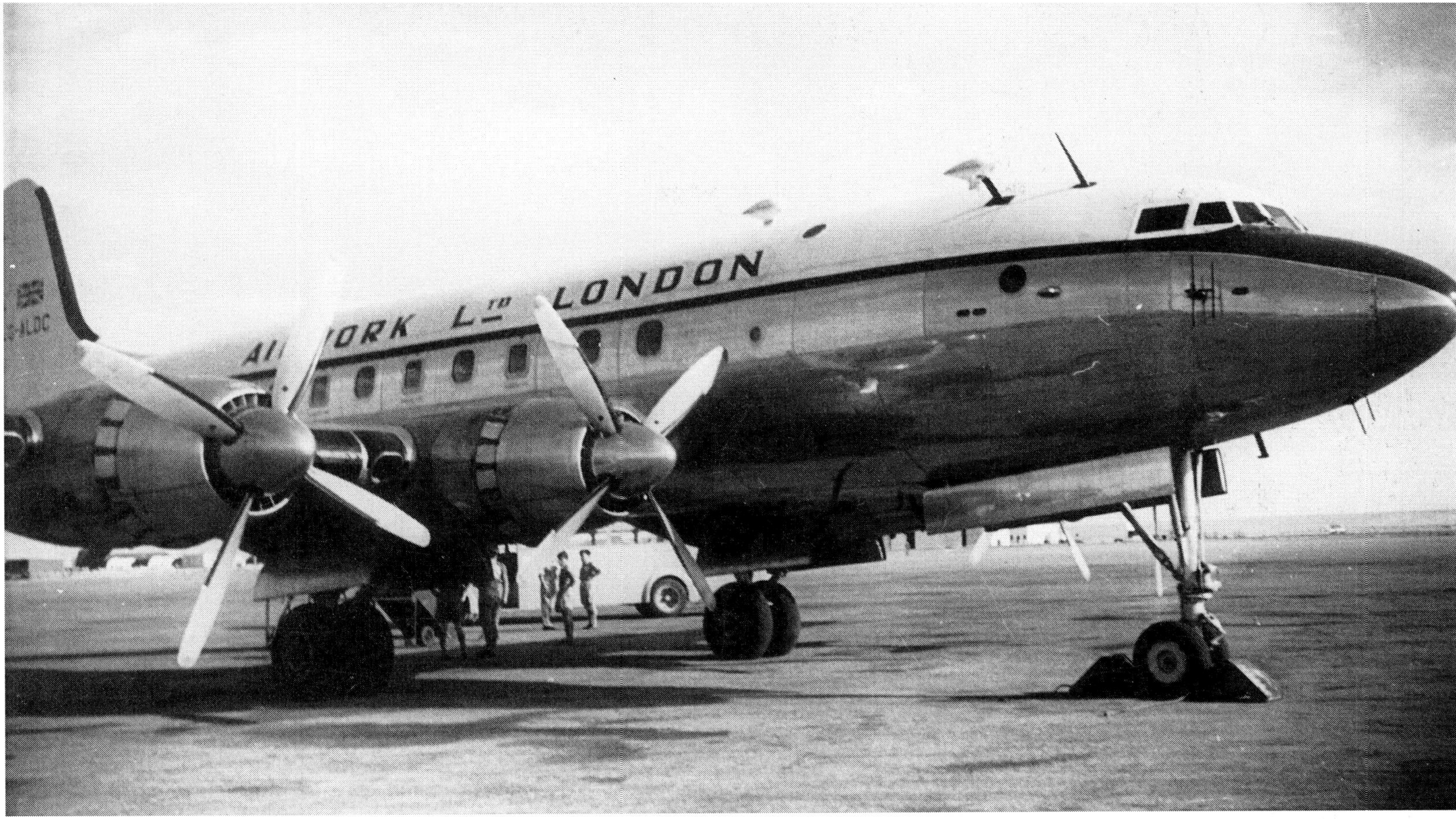

Handley Page Hermes IVA G-ALDC of Airwork Ltd at an eastern aerodrome while probably engaged in trooping work. Karachi Airport was an important staging post for British trooping flights from Britain to Singapore. Airwork was awarded a contract in 1954 to fly British service personnel from Blackbushe Airport, Hampshire, to Singapore using its ex-BOAC Hermes airliners. The first flight was operated by Hermes G-AKFP which left Blackbushe at 10.35am on 3rd October 1954 with 68 servicemen and its ETA at Singapore was 8.35am on 6th October. The route varied according to the weather but included Brindisi, Istanbul, Baghdad, Karachi (night-stop), Delhi, Calcutta and Bangkok. Britavia and Skyways also contributed Hermes for the trooping flights. Almost three years later G-AKFP, which had earlier staged through Karachi and Delhi, was damaged beyond repair after colliding with Indian Airlines' Douglas DC-3 Dakota VT-AUA while landing at Dum Dum Airport, Calcutta, on 1st September 1957. There were no casualties among the Hermes' six crew and 58 passengers but tragically all four occupants of the DC-3 were killed.

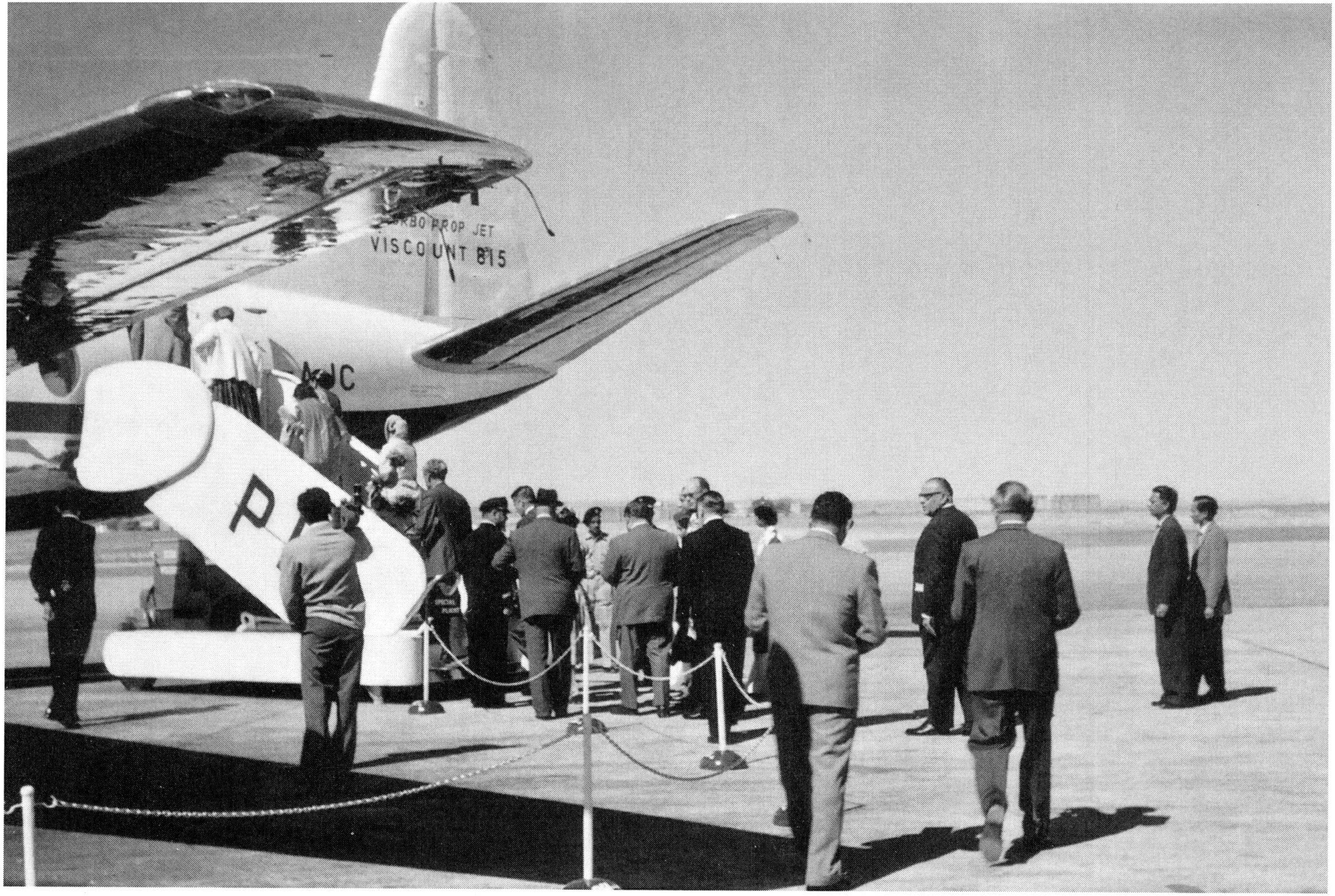

Passengers board Pakistan International Airlines' Vickers Viscount 815 AP-AJC for the inaugural Karachi-Delhi flight on 31st January 1959. The Viscount, powered by four Rolls-Royce Dart turboprops, revolutionised regional air travel throughout much of the world in the 1950s, with Indian Airlines Corporation introducing the type on its Bombay-Karachi route on 10th December 1957. Viscount AP-AJC was later damaged beyond repair after over-running the runway at Rawalpindi on 16th May 1959.

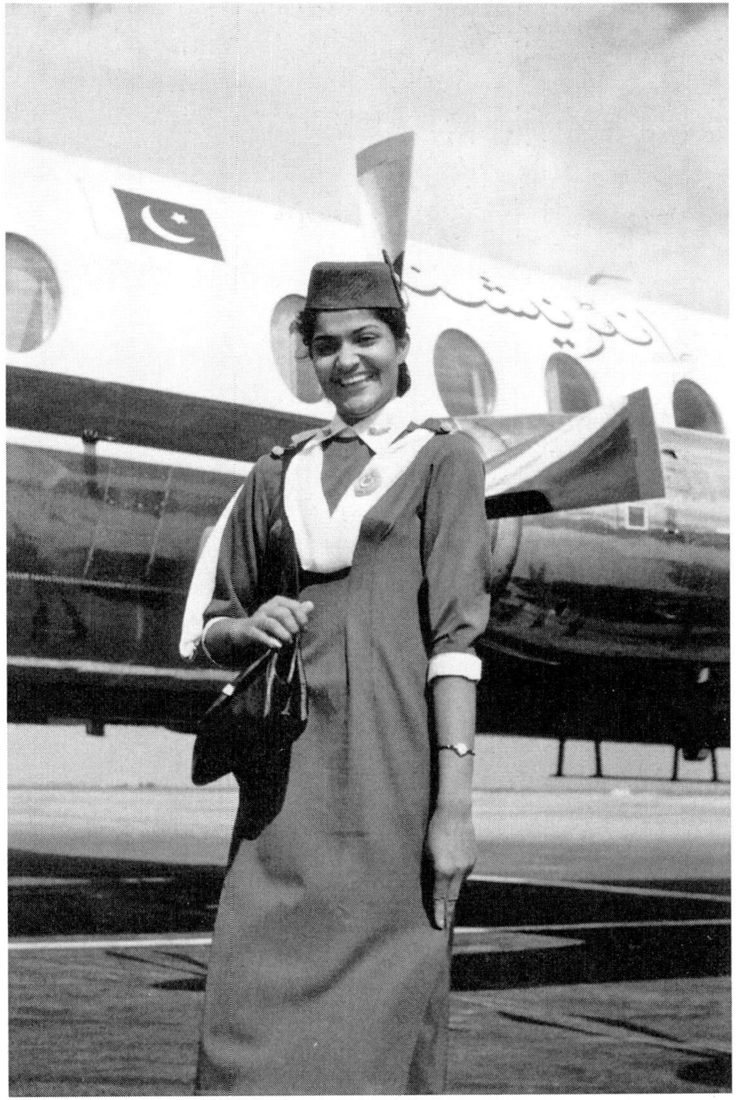

A PIA stewardess poses beside the Viscount before the first jet-prop flight from Karachi to Delhi.

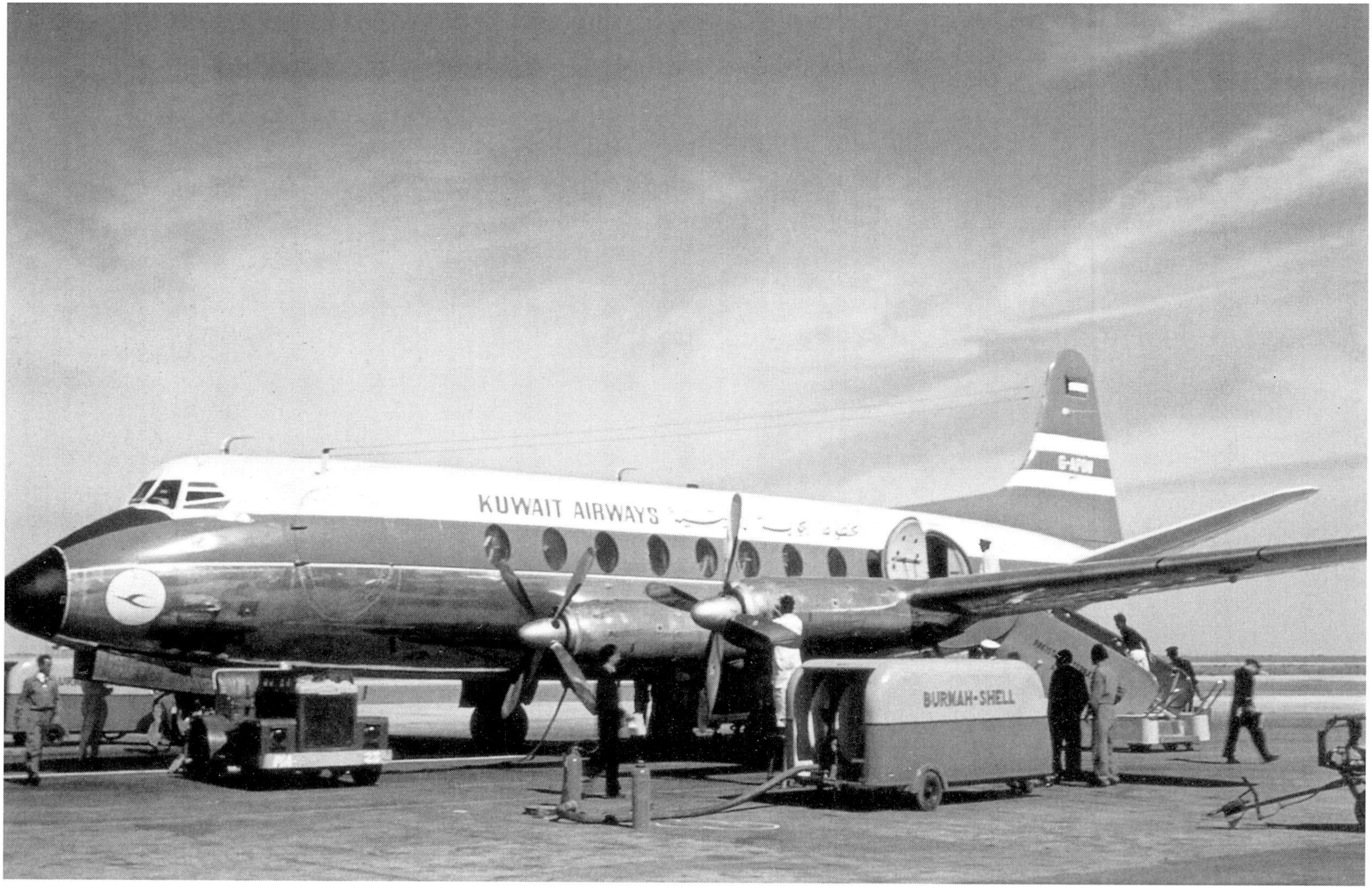

Ground staff attend to Vickers Viscount 702 G-APOW of Kuwait Airways at Karachi Airport in 1960. The airline, which also flew to Bombay, leased it from BOAC Associated Companies from September 1958 until February 1963. This Viscount contributed to a 26% increase in the number of passengers carried by Kuwait Airways in 1960-61.

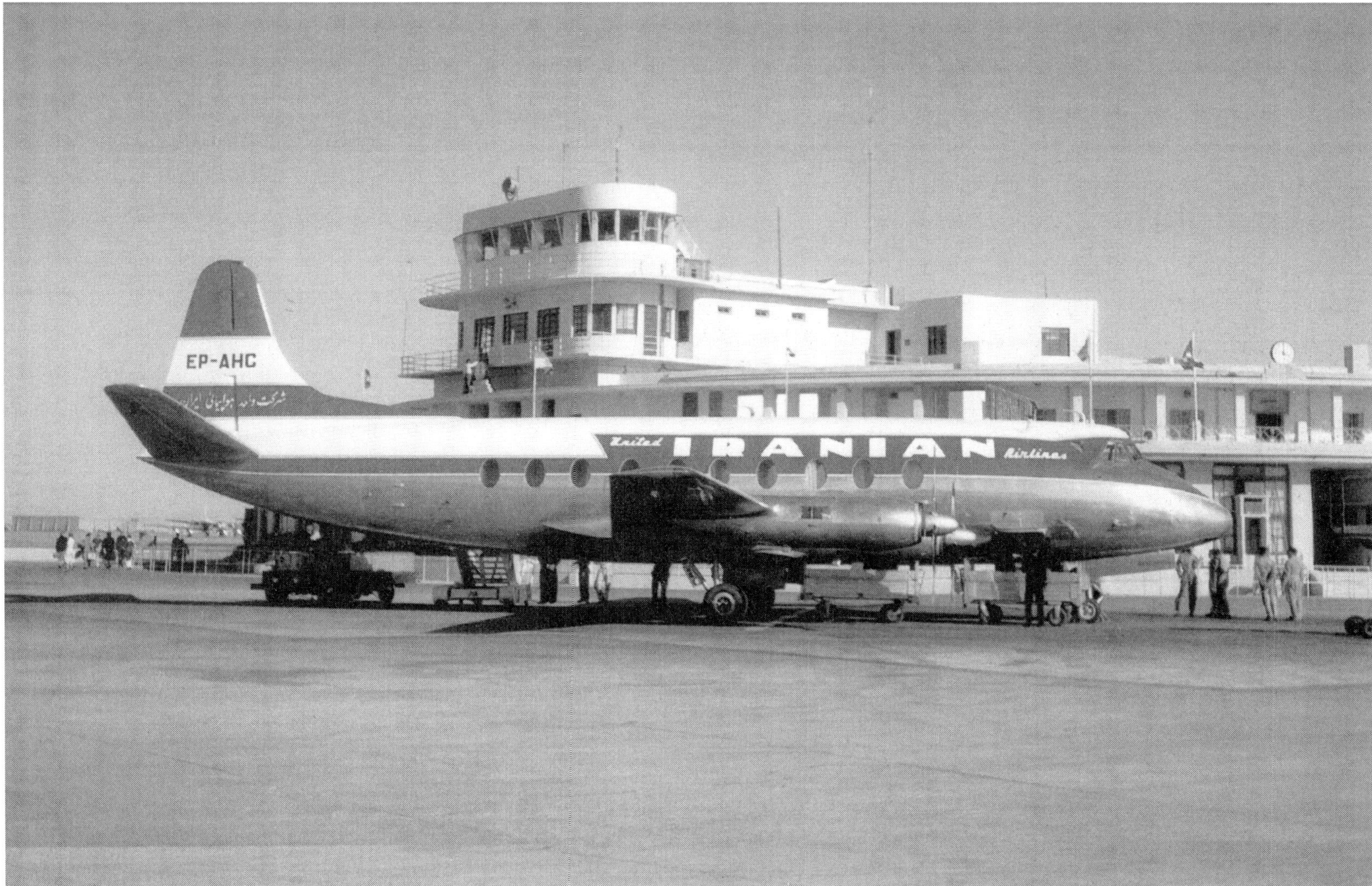

A nostalgic view of United Iranian Airlines' Vickers Viscount 782D EP-AHC at Karachi in 1961 after a scheduled flight from Tehran. It was later damaged beyond repair following a heavy landing at Isfahan, Iran, on 15th February 1965. By the end of 1961, Viscounts had become standard on most inter-city main routes throughout the Middle East.

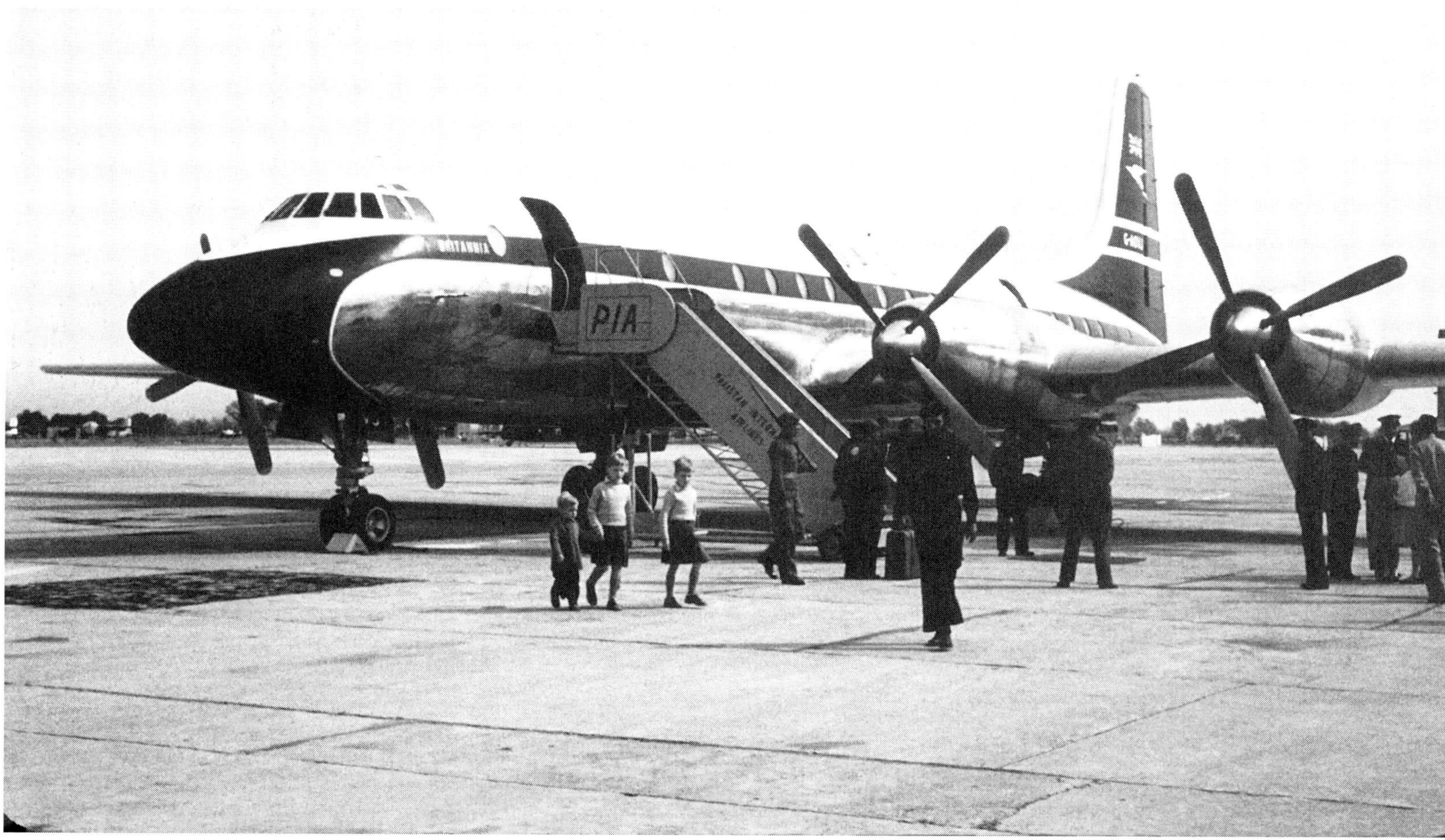

BOAC Bristol Britannia 312 G-AOVJ at Rawalpindi Airport while being used by the Queen and the Duke of Edinburgh during their official tour of Pakistan in February 1961. The royal couple later flew in it to Karachi. Four years earlier, the Britannia had ushered in the turboprop era on BOAC's long-haul routes when series 102 G-ANBK left London-Heathrow on 2nd March 1957 destined for Sydney, Australia, cutting the Constellation time of 56 hours to 47.5. It returned to Heathrow on 9th March, having routed through Darwin, Singapore, Calcutta, Karachi and Istanbul. Four months later, Britannia 102 G-ANBB inaugurated the airline's jet-prop service to Tokyo when it left Heathrow on 16th July routing via Rome, Beirut, Karachi, Calcutta, Rangoon and Hong Kong, arriving at Tokyo at 11.27pm on 18th July. Within about a year, the 15 Britannia 102s ordered were all flying on BOAC's eastern and African routes, where the Whispering Giants, as they were known affectionately, established impressive figures of reliability and a high rate of utilisation.

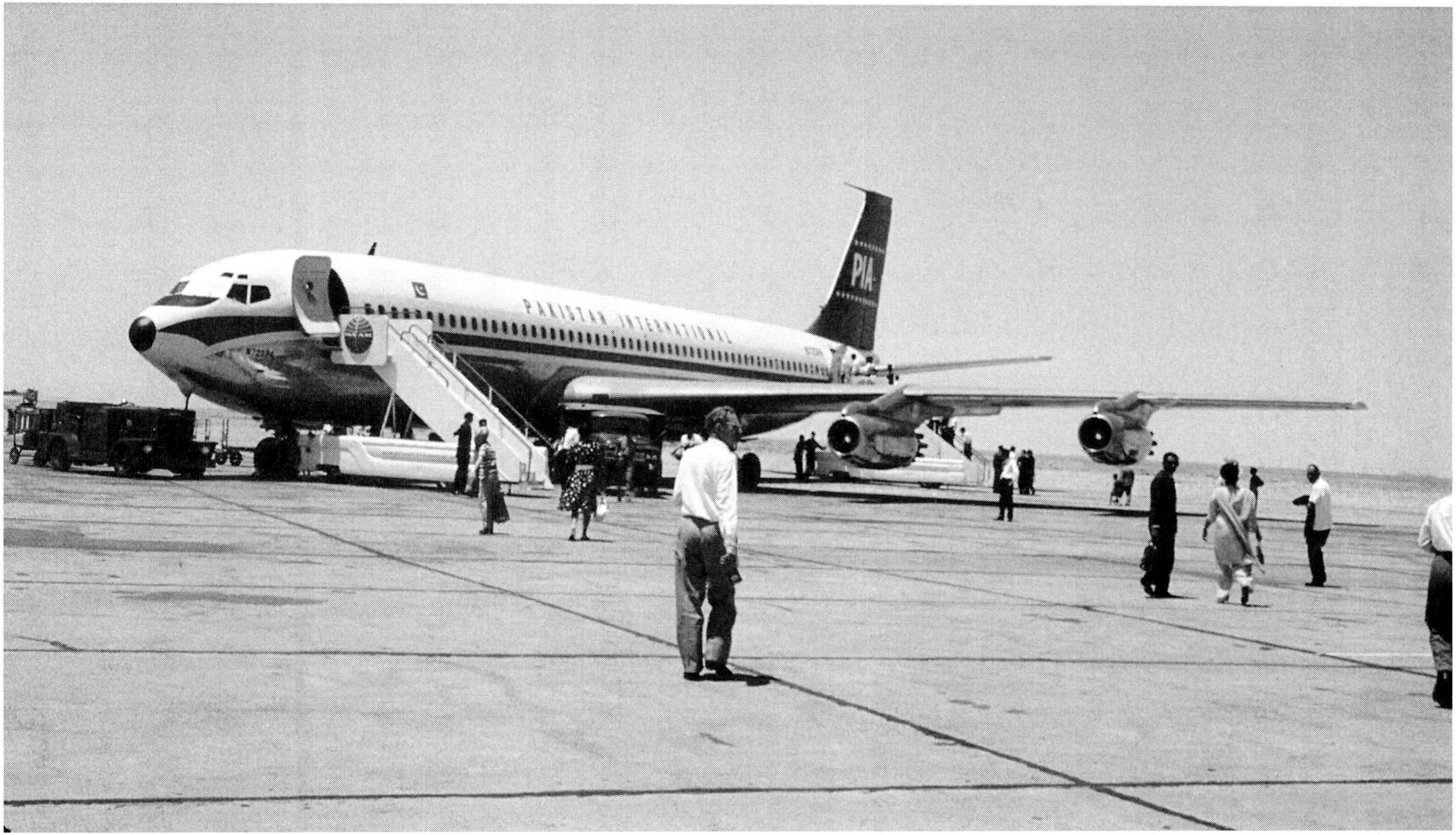

Boeing 707-321 N723PA was leased by Pakistan International Airlines from Pan American World Airways and is seen in 1961 at an intermediate airport where transit passengers were allowed to go for a stroll on the apron, something quite unthinkable in later years for safety and security reasons. It flew PIA's first jet service from London to Karachi, via Rome, Beirut and Tehran, on 7th March 1960. The airline also made history by becoming the first operator of jet airliners in Asia. Aviation journalist John Stroud flew on the inaugural jet service to Karachi and wrote enthusiastically about the Boeing 707's performance in *Flight* magazine (29th April 1960) It had cut the London-Karachi journey time to exactly 12hr compared with 22hr 15min taken by a PIA Super Constellation which made an additional call at Geneva. Stroud predicted PIA would provide some very stiff competition on the Karachi-London route in spite of its fairly limited resources.

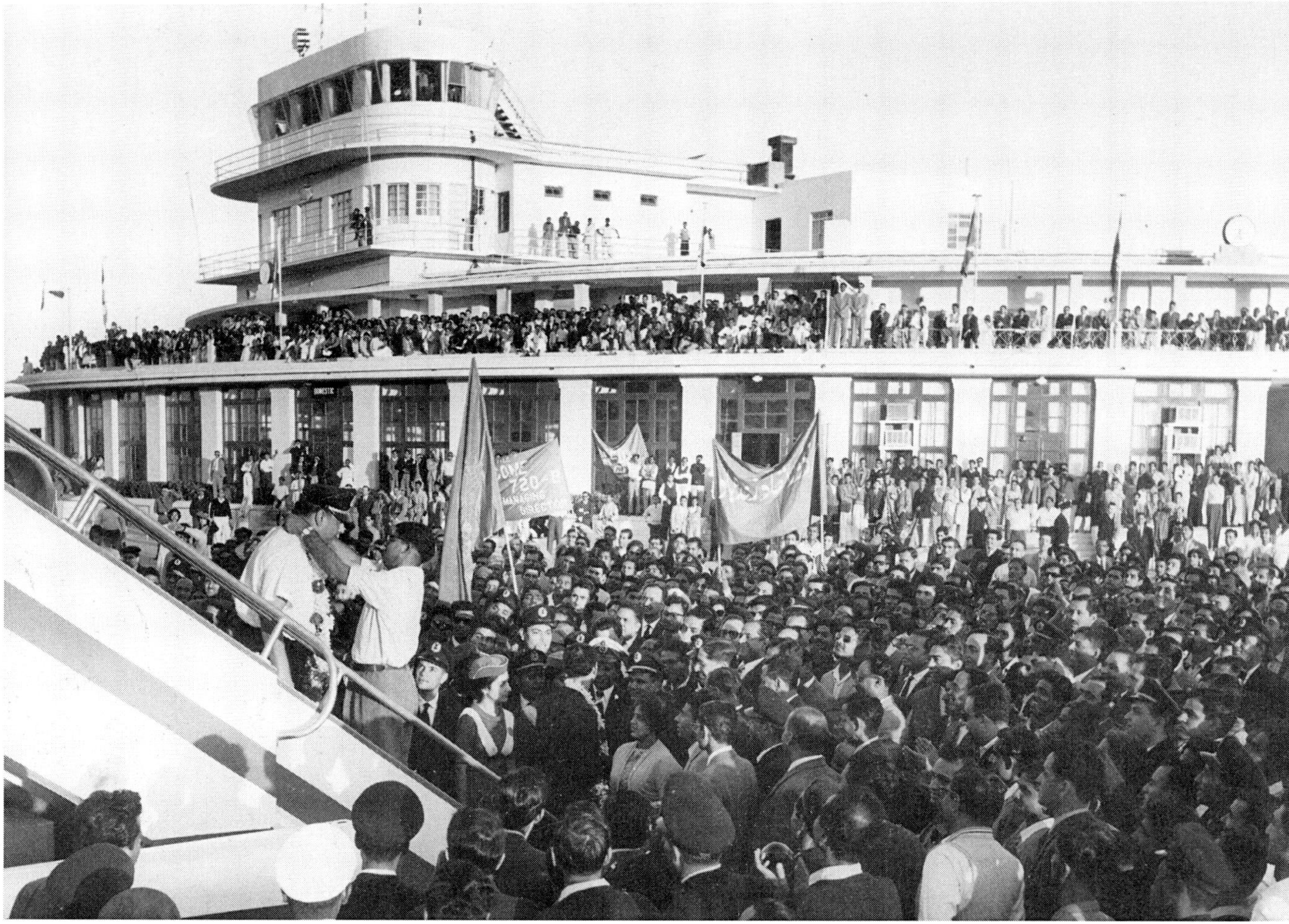

Enthusiastic crowds gather at Karachi Airport to welcome home Pakistan International Airlines' Boeing 720-040B AP-AMG on 2nd January 1962 after its crew created a new flying time record between London and Karachi by covering the distance in 6hr 45min 33sec at an average speed of 583.3 statute miles per hour. PIA chief pilot Captain Abdullah Baig, who captained the Boeing, is seen on the air stairs being garlanded while PIA managing director Air Commodore Malik Nur Khan is at the foot of the stairs. Captain Baig told reporters that the record was broken as a result of the co-ordinated efforts from all crew members on the airliner, adding that it was "the finest team" ever flown by him on any route. The 720B was being delivered from the Boeing factory in Seattle. AP-AMG was joined by two further 720Bs which were used on PIA's Karachi-Dacca route in which they cut the previous flying time by half.

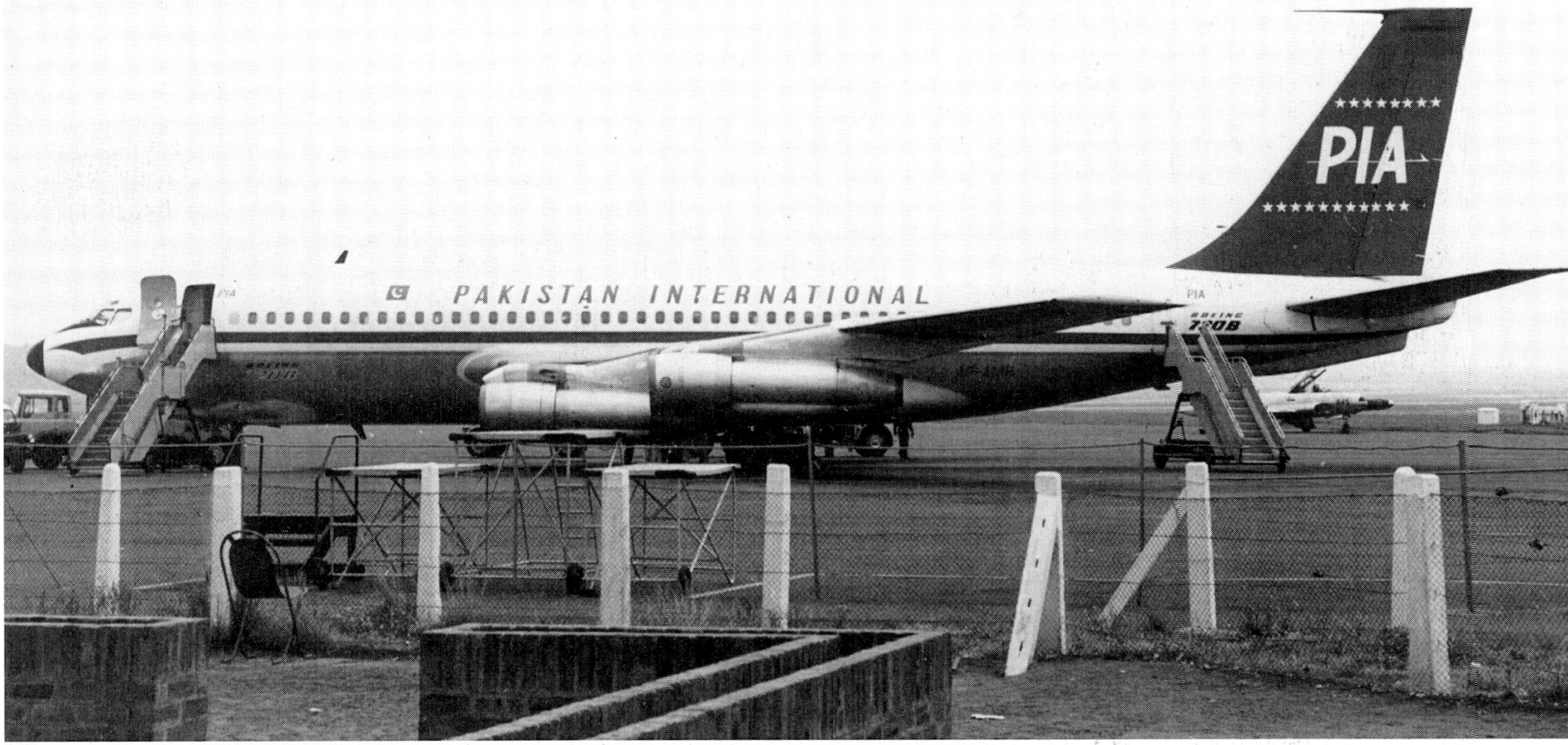

Pakistan International Airlines' Boeing 720B AP-AMH at Prestwick during a delivery flight from the US in November 1962. The airliner was written off following a crash on 20th May 1965. Similar aircraft AP-AXM has been preserved at the PIA Planetarium in Karachi.

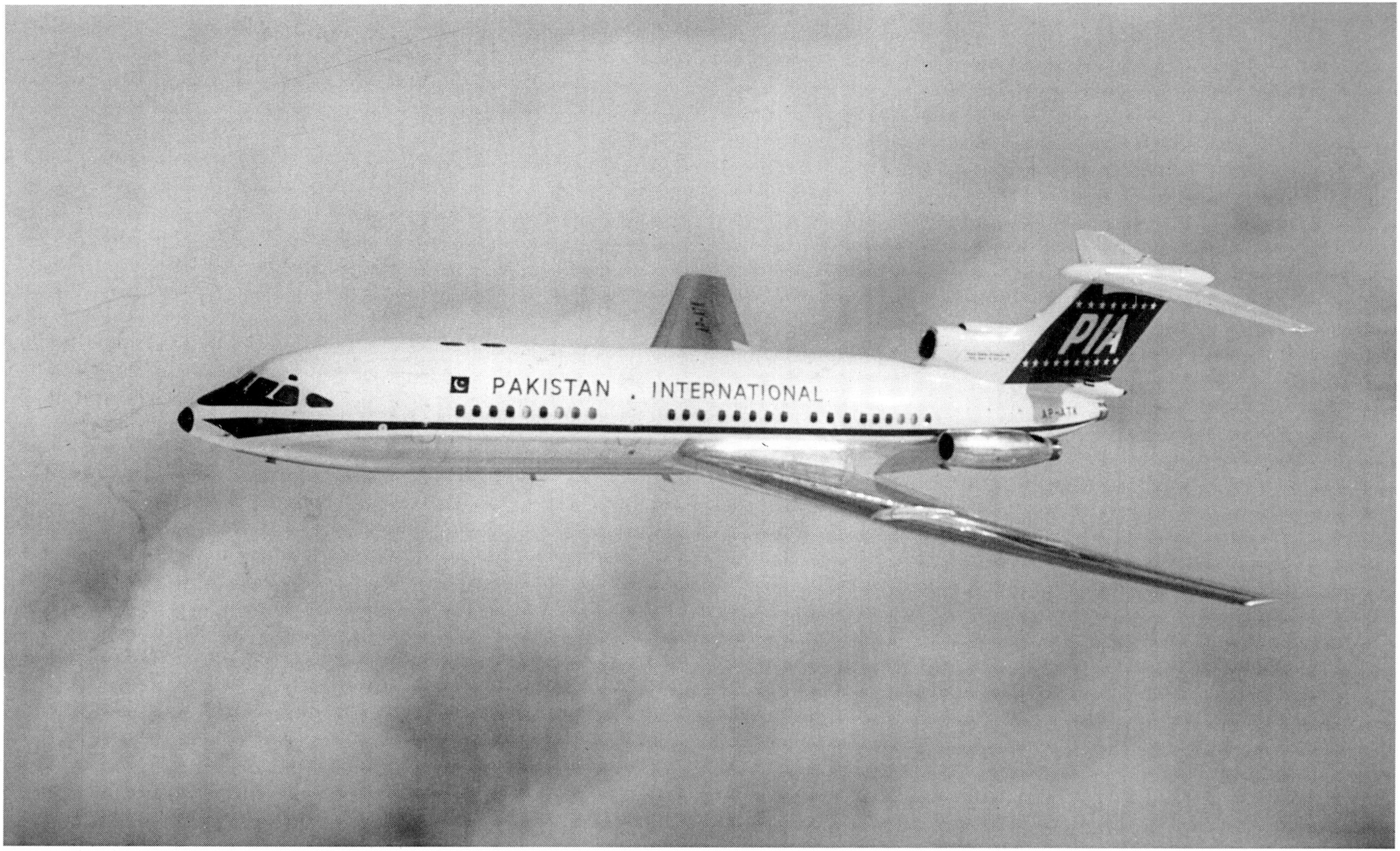

Pakistan International Airlines' Hawker Siddeley Trident 1E AP-ATK was the first of three of the type ordered by the airline and was delivered on 1st March 1966. They were used to link Karachi with Rawalpindi, Lahore and Peshawar, and replaced the three remaining Viscount 815s which were returned to Hawker Siddeley Aviation Ltd in 1966 as part of a trade-in agreement. A fourth Trident was operated by the Pakistan Air Force for VIP flights. The Trident was the last British-designed airliner operated by PIA although it sold its Tridents to the Civil Aviation Administration of China in 1970. The former AP-ATK is now preserved at the China Aviation Museum, Datangshan.